C000229523

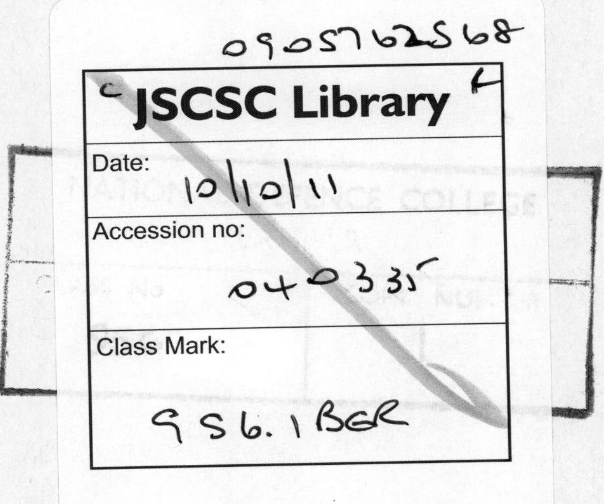
0905762568
JSCSC Library
Date:
10/10/11
Accession no:
040335
Class Mark:
956.1 BER

Turkey in Crisis

From State Capitalism to Neo-colonialism

Berch Berberoglu

Zed Press, 57 Caledonian Road, London N1 9DN.

Turkey in Crisis was first published by Zed Press, 57 Caledonian Road, London N1 9DN in 1982.

Typeset by Margaret Cole
Proofread by Penelope Fryxell
Cover design by Jan Brown Designs
Printed in Great Britain by
Redwood Burn Ltd., Trowbridge, Wiltshire.

British Library Cataloguing in Publication Data

Berberoglu, B.
Turkey in crisis.
1. Turkey – History
I. Title
956.1 DR440
ISBN Hb 0 905762 56 8
Pb 0 905762 61 4

U.S. Distributor
Lawrence Hill and Co., 520 Riverside Avenue, Westport, Conn. 06880, U.S.A.

Note on accents

Due to technical limitations, it was regrettably not possible to insert the various accents on Turkish words.

Contents

Tables

Figures

Acknowledgements

Many of the ideas contained in this book were formed through my participation in numerous seminars, workshops and conferences during my graduate studies at the University of Oregon in the mid-1970s. In this context, I am especially indebted to Al Szymanski, whose ideas have been of decisive influence on my thinking on problems of development, class and revolution in the Third World. I have also benefited from discussions and correspondence with Ismet Guchan, Yildiz Sertel, Hafiz Rahman, and the late Walter Rodney.

I wish to thank Roger van Zwanenberg, Robert Molteno, Ronnie Margolies, Al Szymanski and Ellen Kay Trimberger for providing helpful comments on the manuscript, for without their help this book would not have taken the shape it has today. I would especially like to express my appreciation to Robert Molteno of Zed Press, not only for his technical and detailed substantive assistance during the rewriting stage, but also for his efforts in making the publishing process a pleasant one. Finally, I would like to thank my wife Suzan for her continuous intellectual support at every stage in the preparation of this manuscript.

Special thanks are also due to Carol MacKenzie for her skillful typing of the final draft of the manuscript.

B. Berberoglu
Reno, Nevada, USA
April 1981

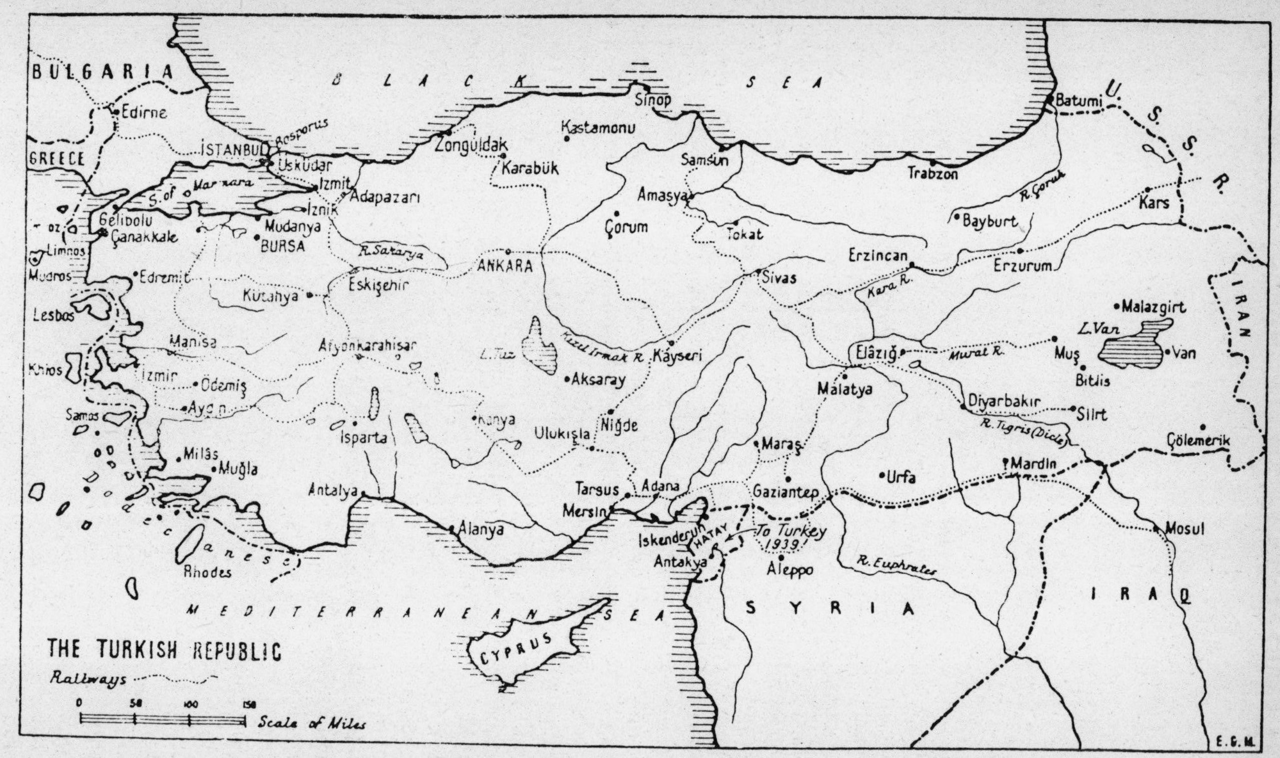

THE TURKISH REPUBLIC

Railways

0 50 100 150 Scale of Miles

Introduction

This book is a study in the political economy of state capitalism in the Third World as applied to the case of Turkey. It examines the Turkish case as a classic example of a post The Great Depression state capitalist formation in the Third World during the second quarter of this century and traces its transformation into a neo-colonial state in the period since World War II.

Starting with an analysis of the origins and formation of the modern Turkish state, Chapter One presents an account of the social and economic structure of the Ottoman Empire and the role of the Ottoman state in the production process. It outlines the class structure of Turkey at the time of the disintegration of the Ottoman social formation at the end of the 19th and the beginning of the 20th centuries, and examines the class forces behind the war of national liberation which led to the formation of the new Turkish state in 1923. Chapter Two examines the nature and extent of state intervention in the national economy in the 1920s and explicates the economic policies of the Kemalist state, both in agriculture and in industry, during this period. Chapter Three focuses on the process of national industrialization throughout the 1930s and probes the dynamics of state capitalist development in Turkey during this period. It also discusses the nationalization of foreign firms, the First and Second Five Year Industrial Development Plans, the role of state banks in the industrialization process, developments in the agricultural sector, and the balance of trade. Chapter Four is devoted to an analysis of the underlying internal and external contradictions of the state capitalist regime during the 1930s and 1940s and examines the nature of class contradictions and class struggles throughout this period. The extent of exploitation and oppression of the working class and the peasantry, the severity of the struggle between the state and the landlords and compradors, and the latter's ultimately successful attempt – in collusion with imperialism – to transform Turkey into a neo-colonial dependency, are also examined in this chapter.

In Chapter Five the focus is on the political economy of dependent, neo-colonial development in the 1950s – a period marking the consolidation of the power of big landlords and the comprador bourgeoisie. This period also marks the intensification of exploitation and oppression of the working class and the peasantry and, in response to it, the growth of a mass popular movement which helped bring the overthrow, through a military coup, of the Bayar-Menderes regime. Chapter Six examines the nature and implications of the coup d'etat of May 1960, party politics and coalition governments in the 1960s, the consolidation of neo-colonialism and developments in the neo-colonial economy, the condition of the working class and the development of independent trade union and political organization among workers and peasants and the emerging class struggle at the end of the decade. Finally, Chapter Seven examines the 1971 military intervention and the nature of military rule during 1971–73, the 1973 elections and post–1973 coalition governments, the faltering neo-colonial economy's performance in the 1970s, the condition of the working class and the class struggle during this period and the intensification of the class struggle and the revolutionary situation at the end of the decade.

Through an analysis of the development and transformation of state capitalism in Turkey from the 1930s to the 1950s, this study shows the process by which the contradictions of the state capitalist formation have led to the restoration of neo-colonialism in Turkey in the post-World War II period to the present. While this analysis of the Turkish experience provides further evidence of the long-term impossibility of independent, national state capitalist development in the Third World, it also leads to the conclusion that only through socialism can imperialism be expelled and capitalism abolished.

1. The Formation of the Turkish State

At the start of the 20th Century, Turkey, or the Ottoman Empire as it was then, was an overwhelmingly rural society, with very little large-scale productive activity in industry. While it never became a formal colony of the expanding European powers throughout its long and turbulent history, the central government of the Ottoman Empire was in many ways vulnerable to external pressures from the West. The European powers, taking advantage of the endless wars in the Empire's various provinces, found their way in, first through indirect economic domination from the 17th to the mid-19th Centuries and, subsequently, through direct economic controls and military occupation of large parts of Ottoman territory at the end of the 19th and beginning of the 20th Centuries. This culminated in the occupation of virtually every corner of the Empire during World War I.

These final stages of Ottoman history (encompassing the period from the 'Young Turk' Revolution of 1908 to the imperialist occupation of Turkey during World War I) witnessed the resurgence of Turkish nationalism. Promoted by patriotic forces from among the Ottoman intelligentsia and the Officer Corps headed by Mustafa Kemal, this was later to result in the struggle for the formation of the new Turkish state. However, before analysing the events surrounding the formation of the Turkish state, it is worth tracing the main developments in the historical process marking the final decades of the Ottoman Empire at the end of the 19th and the beginning of the 20th Centuries.

Decline of the Ottoman Empire

The centuries-old Empire of the Ottomans, which at its peak extended from Asia Minor to Vienna, from Palestine to Algeria and down to the Persian Gulf in Mesopotamia in the late 17th century, began to face serious economic and politico-military problems during the 18th and 19th centuries. The expanding power of local landowners and merchants linked to European commercial capital, peasant uprisings and wars of national liberation throughout the Empire, loss of territory as a result of military defeats in Europe and elsewhere, the decline of native industry and increasing dependence on the capitalist West and expanding public debt were all major factors contributing to the process of disintegration of the Ottoman Empire.[1]

The growth and expansion of tax-farming (*iltizam*) and the development of Ottoman commerce which, as it extended into the international sphere, acquired an intermediary function between local landowners and European commercial capital, contributed to: (1) the weakening of the authority of the central state *vis-a-vis* the new propertied and moneyed classes in the countryside; and (2) the establishment of direct economic ties with European capital which, as we shall see later, became the basis of the expansion of Western capitalism into the Empire's economy.[2]

The growing power of local landowners on the one hand, and increasing repression by the central state on the other, did not go unchallenged. The oppressed peasants and minority nationalities in various parts of the Empire rose up in arms.

The peasant uprisings of the 17th century (*Celali Isyanlari*)[3] continued in varied forms during the 18th and 19th centuries. Although these revolts did not yield substantial results in terms of the transformation of the agrarian structure, they did nonetheless create an unstable situation for both the peasantry's local exploiters and the central state, which made it possible to grant occasional concessions in favour of the peasant masses.

National minorities, especially in the Balkans, waged battle against the repressive, despotic state to gain their independence. As a result of the prolonged wars with the European powers, which extended from the second siege of Vienna (1683) to the Treaty of Jassy (1792), the Ottoman state became more and more vulnerable, leading to massive territorial losses that included Hungary, Greece, Transylvania, Bukovina, the northern coasts of the Black Sea, Crimea, and other regions.[4] This, in turn, encouraged indigenous nationalist forces to rise up and put an end to Ottoman rule over their territories. By the 19th century the Ottoman state faced serious challenge from every corner of the Empire: Serbia, Egypt, North Africa, Eastern Anatolia, and elsewhere.[5] The successful revolts of the colonized peoples reduced the area of plunder by the central state and the Ottoman lords. This contraction of the Empire exacerbated the crises in the Ottoman economy and polity and further contributed to its decline.

While the Ottoman state was becoming rapidly weaker and its influence in the Mediterranean suffered continual erosion, Europe had completed its transition from feudalism to capitalism.[6] Thus, by the late 18th century, Europe's old (feudal) economy had been transformed by the expanding capitalist mode, which spread with increasing vigour to the Mediterranean region and elsewhere in pursuit of raw materials and new markets. Growing trade between Western Europe and Ottoman Turkey during this period began to have adverse effects on local, small-scale Ottoman industry. Faced with rising costs and operating under strict price regulations, the Ottoman guilds were unable to provide goods at prices low enough to compete with the cheap European-manufactured goods that entered the Empire without restriction, due to the Capitulation Agreements.[7] Consequently, traditional Ottoman industry entered a period of rapid decline and the Empire became more and more dependent on the European economies.

As European capital began to expand, there was no longer a need to depend on imports of manufactured goods from the East, as had been the case earlier. In fact, the growing capitalist economy in Europe, now able to take full advantage of the favourable terms provided by the Capitulations, was in a position to bring about a complete reversal in international trade. Whereas England was previously an importer of textiles from the East, she now became an *exporter* of these. Thus, for example, while the value of exports of cotton fabrics from England to Turkey as only £10,834 in 1828, they rose to £39,920 in 1829, to £95,355 in 1830 and to £105,615 in 1831 – a tenfold increase in just four years.[8] The process of British (and other European) expansion into the Ottoman economy accelerated even more following the Anglo-Turkish Commercial Convention of 1838, for it extended extra-territorial privileges to all foreign traders and abolished the state's protective tariffs and monopolies.[9] Consequently, whereas the Ottoman Empire had supplied almost all of Britain's cotton fabric imports in 1825 (30,533 kg), by 1855 this amount had fallen sharply to a point where it constituted only a fraction of these imports (1,506 kg).[10] British exports to Turkey continued to expand in the post-Convention period, with the result that cotton fabric imports by the Ottoman Empire rose from 15,846,678 metres in 1835 to 121,254,439 metres in 1855; silk fabric imports rose from 20,898 kg in 1835 to 81,286 kg in 1855; linen fabric imports rose from 33,807 kg in 1835 to 599,148 kg in 1855; and woollen fabric imports rose from 52,819 kg in 1835 to 906,602 kg in 1855.[11] This reversal in the import-export pattern of the Empire led to the destruction of the textile industry in Ottoman Turkey.

Local yarn production and silk and cotton fabric weaving declined dramatically: in Albania, the number of looms in operation dropped from 600 in 1812 to 40 in 1821; in Tirnova, from 2,000 in 1812 to 200 in 1830; in Bursa, from 1,000 down to 75, with a reduction in use of raw silk from 25,000 *okkas* to 4,000 *okkas.*[12] According to a report issued in 1868 by the Industrial Improvement Commission, the number of cloth-producing looms in Istanbul and Uskudar during the preceding thirty or forty years had collapsed from 2,750 to 25; the number of brocade looms from 350 to 4; and the number of upholstery silk looms from 60 to 8.[13] According to numerous other reports, the situation was similar in even remote parts of the Empire (e.g. Aleppo and Mosul).[14] While the process of dismantling native Ottoman industry by the British had begun in the textiles sector in the early 19th century, all other branches of Ottoman industry had become affected in a few short decades so that by the late 1800s the whole of Ottoman industry was on the verge of collapse.[15]

These developments marked the end of industrialization via the manufacturing sector in Ottoman Turkey, and the Empire was instead relegated to raw materials production geared to the needs of the European-dominated world economy. Hence, cotton production rose from 400 tons in 1896 to

33,750 tons in 1914; the area under tobacco expanded from 192,262 *donum* in 1884 to 814,162 *donum* in 1911; and tobacco production rose from 22.5 million kg. to 63.5 million kg. during the same period.[16]

Increases occurred in other agricultural products as well, such as raisins and dried figs, whose output nearly doubled during the nine-year period 1904–13.[17] Thus, instead of using its agriculture as a base for internal industrial expansion, as to some extent had been the case up to the 19th century, the Ottoman Empire, with its native industry destroyed, was transformed into an agrarian reserve of the expending European capitalist economies.[18]

This process, coupled with continued territorial losses throughout the Empire, frustrated the state's efforts to raise revenue for the public treasury. While increased taxation was seen as a short-term remedy to counteract these tendencies,[19] the only long-term 'solution' to the problem of revenue was seen to be foreign loans.[20]

The first Ottoman foreign loan was in 1854, and by 1877 the nominal public debt was £190,997,980 (plus interest amounting to £61,803,905), with annual interest and amortization payments taking £12,000,000, or more than half the national revenue.[21] By 1877 the Ottoman state was no longer able to continue its loan repayments, and, consequently, it declared bankruptcy. A European-controlled organization, the Ottoman Public Debt Administration (OPDA), was set up in 1881 to collect payments on the loans.[22] The OPDA subsequently acted as an intermediary with European companies seeking investment opportunities in Turkey and in this way was instrumental in facilitating the further penetration of European capital into the Ottoman economy.[23]

By the 19th century, then, Ottoman Turkey had for all practical purposes become a semi-colony of the expanding European powers. Its economy was mortgaged to foreign capitalists and their states, widespread revolts had occurred throughout its conquered territories, and new social groups had emerged which, by the middle of the century, were already posing problems for its continued, if ill-fated, existence under the rule of the Sultanate and the Palace bureaucracy.

It is in this context that progressive forces began to emerge and address themselves to the pressing problems facing the Ottoman state and society.

Resurgence of Turkish Nationalism

Nationalist uprisings occurred in this period in Crete (1896–97) and Macedonia (1903). But the most far-reaching developments were those connected with the 'Young Turk' Revolution (1908).[24]

In Istanbul military students exposed to European ideas were discontented with the despotic Ottoman state. Nationalist ideas were put forward by numerous intellectuals and journalists, the most prominent of whom was Namik Kemal. Abdul-Hamid II, the ruling Sultan, tried to suppress the movement by arrests, forced exile and executions, but without success. Secret societies were formed in Army Headquarters throughout the Empire and in Paris, Geneva and Cairo. The most effective of these became the Committee of Union and Progress, or the 'Young Turks'.[25]

Finally, in 1908, there was discontent within the Third Army Corps in Macedonia. On July 4, 1908, the Army, headed by Major Ahmed Niyazi, demanded from Salonika in Macedonia the restoration of the 1876 Constitution and marched on Istanbul.[26] The Sultan's attempt to suppress the rising failed, and rebellion spread rapidly. Unable to rely on other troops, on July 23 Abdul-Hamid II announced the restoration of the Constitution.[27] Elections were held and a constitutional government was established. But in April 1909 Abdul-Hamid II struck back with a counter-revolution and the Army moved up again from Macedonia to depose the Sultan and install his brother, Mehmed V, as constitutional monarch.

The Committee of Union and Progress, which led the 1908 Young Turk Revolution, declared itself to be a political party – the Party of Union and Progress (PUP) – in April 1909 and took power through the elections of April 1912.[28] The top leadership of the Party was mainly composed of Turkish intellectuals who were to a great extent influenced by European progressive and nationalist thought at the end of the 19th century. Their essentially petty-bourgeois ideology and nationalist policy brought them in line with their main class allies, namely 'the *esnaf* (artisans) and the *tuccar* (merchants) of the towns – the class out of which the PUP sought to forge a Turkish bourgeoisie'.[29] Hence, it was in this context, and after the massive territorial losses following the two Balkan Wars (1912–13)[30] and the failure of the ruling PUP clique to safeguard Turkey from the onslaught of imperialist occupation forces during the First World War, that the stage was set for the emergence of Mustafa Kemal and the Kemalists who came to assume the leadership of the liberation forces. To understand the origin and the evolution of the Nationalist offensive, it is necessary to examine the social and class structure of Turkey during this period and examine the balance of class forces at the time of the liberation struggle.

Social and Class Structure of Turkey in the Late 19th Century

For centuries the dominant mode of production in the Ottoman formation had been the 'Asiatic mode of production'.[31] Interaction between the Ottoman formation and Byzantine society developed after the invasion of Constantinople by the Ottoman forces in 1453. This interaction, as well as that with other European formations following Ottoman expansion into Europe in the 15th and 16th centuries, and the state's land allocation system (*timar*),[32] eventually led to the development of feudal forms in Ottoman agriculture (*iltizam* or tax-farming) where, over time, large-scale private property in land (*ciftlik*) acquired increasing importance, transferring a high proportion of the land to a few owners.[33] While the position of landlords was strengthened as a result of this process initiated by the state, interaction with Europe also facilitated the expansion of European commercial capital into the Empire, leading to the development of a comprador class tied to European imperialism. However, the development, first, of feudalism in agriculture and, later, capitalism in commerce and industry, took place within the confines of a society dominated by the Asiatic state which permitted the coexistence of these diverse modes until the very end.[34]

To gain greater insight into the nature and transformation of the Ottoman social formation in the early 20th century, it is necessary to take account of the structure of class forces dominating the Empire's economy and polity during this (final) phase of its development.

(1) Political power in the Empire rested in the throne of the central authority, the *Padisah* or Sultan, and his administrative deputy called the *Sadrazam* or Grand Vezir. Below this, and under the direct control of the Sultan, there existed the large but carefully organized Ottoman Palace bureaucracy.[35] It was largely the corrupt and adventurist practices of the Sultan and the Palace bureaucracy in the latter phase of the Ottomans' centuries-long imperial history that transformed the Empire into a semi-colony of the expanding world capitalist economy. It was this (political) structure that clashed – first in 1908 and again a decade later – with nationalist forces led by the Unionist and, later, the Kemalist petty bourgeoisie.

(2) The dominant economic interests in Ottoman Turkey during this period were made up of a grouping of big landowners (the *ayans, derebeys,* and *agas*) in the countryside and comprador capitalists of mainly minority ethnic origin in major urban centres. In 1913, the traditional landed gentry (the *ayans* and *derebeys*), together with the *agas,* constituted 5% of the farmer families and owned 65% of the arable land. As a result of their vast economic power in the countryside, the big landowners were able to monopolize local political power and, through links with the rural Islamic clergy, impose their social and cultural domination over the peasantry. The subjugation of the peasant masses by the landlord-clergy coalition (the *esraf*) thus served the double function of exploitation and legitimization.

(3) Largely involved in import-export trade and domestic marketing tied to European imports, the minority commercial interests – comprised of Greek and Armenian merchants and primarily concentrated in large urban centres such as Istanbul and Izmir – made up the basis of the Empire's comprador bourgeoisie.[36] The role of minority compradors has been pivotal in two contradictory respects. First, through their key position in the urban economy they were in effect the agency for external economic penetration and control, which contributed to the final demise of the Empire's Asiatic mode of production in its evolution into more advanced socio-economic forms. Second, their parasitic position in the economy, *vis-a-vis* national industrial development, hindered the transition to the (industrial) capitalist mode of production. Consequently, on balance, while their strategic role in accelerating contact with the West played a progressive role in the admittedly

limited transformation of the Asiatic mode in an earlier period, the continued existence of the minority bourgeoisie as a comprador class – as opposed to their transformation into industrial capitalists – perpetuated the backward and dependent structure of Ottoman industry and contributed instead to the further dependence of the Ottoman economy on European capital through debt bondage and as supplier of raw materials, which assisted the development of capitalism in Western Europe. It is this latter, parasitic and anti-developmental role of Greek and Armenian comprador agents of European imperialism that in good part gave rise to the nationalist movement of the Society of Union and Progress and to the Kemalist forces in the war of national liberation.

(4) Closely linked with this minority comprador group and the Palace bureaucracy was foreign finance capital or the imperialist bourgeoisie. The penetration into Ottoman Turkey of imperialist finance capital during this period was based on the Empire's role as a raw materials-supplying semi-colony of the expanding European economy. Concentrated largely in the raw materials sector, foreign capital was also engaged in the construction of a network of railways in Western and Central Anatolia, with the sole purpose of accelerating the process of raw materials extraction in Turkey.[37] The absence of the development to any significant degree of European manufacturing industries in Ottoman Turkey was 'compensated' for by the flow into the Empire of European goods that were handled through the intermediary of the minority comprador bourgeoisie. Hence, it was in this classic sense – as an exporter of raw materials and importer of finished goods – that the Ottoman Empire became, in essence, a *de facto,* dependent semi-colony.[38]

(5) The dependent structure of the Ottoman economy during the 19th century, coupled with its tributary position in the Mediterranean economy encompassing the period since the early 16th century, did not permit the development of large-scale local industry. Consequently, there never developed a full-blown class of industrialists that would resemble the classical European national industrial bourgeoisie.[39] While a limited expansion did take place in small-scale manufacturing and processing industries, it was largely the minority comprador bourgeoisie that, in addition to its traditional place in commerce, extended into the ownership and control of these industries[40] and prospered under the terms of the Empire's dependent economy. The small number of ethnic Turkish firms that operated in Ottoman Turkey at the time, however, had interests that were diametrically opposed to those of the imperialist and minority bourgeoisies. Although weak in numbers and economic strength, the political aspirations of Turkish industrialists coincided with and took expression in the leadership of the Nationalist forces as their economic position began to deteriorate with the further expansion into industry and trade of the metropolitan and minority bourgeoisies. It was this deterioration in the position of the Turkish national bourgeoisie that later drove its members on to the side of the Nationalist leadership in the struggle against the forces of imperialism and reaction, represented mainly by the Palace and the minority comprador bourgeoisie.

(6) Given the limited size and restricted nature of both national and foreign-owned local industry, the size of the working class was also small: in 1915, the number of workers employed in the industrial sector totalled only 13,485.[41] Moreover, the ethnic composition of the working class was highly fragmented[42] and did not allow for the development of working-class unity:

> The small, specifically Turkish segment of the working class was not only scattered among many small establishments, and not only isolated politically and culturally from the overwhelming majority of Turks who remained on the land as peasants, it was also culturally and politically isolated from the non-Turkish segments of the working class.[43]

This split within the working class reached its peak during the liberation struggles when non-Turkish workers identified with and joined the ranks of the forces of their own ethnic groups and fought against the forces of Turkish national liberation. Isolated as they were in Istanbul and Izmir – the main centres of industry which came under the control of foreign occupation forces during the liberation struggle – Turkish workers were cut off from Anatolia and could not contribute directly to or affect the outcome of the national liberation struggle. Thus several factors – mainly the numerical inferiority, ethnic heterogeneity, and geographical isolation of the Ottoman working class – held back the workers from direct participation in the National Front, which otherwise might well have influenced the direction and outcome of the liberation struggle.

(7) In the Turkish countryside, the majority of the rural population consisted of small-holding peasants. Dispersed throughout the Anatolian interior and engaged in subsistence agriculture, the Turkish peasantry was under the direct control of big landowners who exercised economic, political and cultural domination over them through links with the rural Islamic clergy.[44] While 1% of farmer families in 1913 accounted for 3,000,000 hectares (or 39%) of arable land, 87% of farmer families had access to only 2,700,000 hectares (or 35%) of arable land.[45] This disparity in wealth and economic position did not, however, lead to the radicalization of the small-holding peasantry; neither did it ensure its voluntary participation in the national liberation struggle. Although objectively occupying a revolutionary position in terms of its class interests, the Turkish peasantry, given the enormous economic and political power and socio-religious control exercised over them by the dominant *esraf*, was unable to develop revolutionary class consciousness and transform the agrarian structure through united class action. Despite the grip of the landlords and the clergy over the peasant masses throughout Turkey, there were a number of mass peasant uprisings in Ottoman-Turkish history (e.g. *Celali Isyanlari*) which challenged the rule of the *esraf* and the traditional landed gentry.

(8) Finally, in addition to the small-holding peasantry, rural Turkey also contained a class of small merchants and local artisans, who, together with

doctors, lawyers, teachers and locally based government officials, made up the core of the Anatolian petty bourgeoisie.[46] It was in this intermediate group that the Kemalist forces first found their crucial support in laying the basis of their national campaign among the masses of the Anatolian peasantry. Dominated and controlled by imperialism and the minority bourgeoisie in the urban centres and oppressed under the rule of the *ayan*, the *derebey*, and the *esraf* in the countryside, the Ottoman petty bourgeoisie was highly fragmented, weak and lacked an organizational base to consolidate its power to serve its own class interests in national politics.

Moreover, the lack of an organizational link between the urban and the rural areas among the different sections of the petty bourgeoisie was a major obstacle to the development of petty-bourgeois class solidarity throughout Ottoman Turkey. Among the different strata of this class, it was the sections associated with the various bureaucratic organizations of the state – above all, junior army officers and nationalist intellectuals and journalists, who in an earlier period had embraced Unionist politics and had participated in the Young Turk nationalist movement – that emerged as the top leadership of the NLF and became the Kemalists' organizational core. Central and North-eastern Anatolia became the centre of the resistance movement, and by May 1919, which marks the landing of M. Kemal in Samsun, the Liberation War was under way.

The War of National Liberation and Its Class Alliances

Cognizant of the prevailing conditions in Ottoman Turkey during this period, the Kemalist leadership realized that the main enemy – imperialism – needed to be defeated through armed struggle on three tactical fronts: the imperialist occupation forces;[47] the Ottoman Palace forces with its corrupt and despotic state; and the minority comprador bourgeoisie. Given the heavy concentration of enemy forces in the major urban areas (primarily in Istanbul and Izmir), the Kemalist leadership withdrew to the Turkish countryside in mid-1919 to organize and wage the national liberation struggle through guerrilla warfare.

The immediate task of the Nationalist leadership was to put together fighting forces throughout Anatolia to wage a full-scale offensive against the main enemy and its internal agents. While the big landowners and the clergy had collaborated with the Palace and imperialist occupation forces in their areas, the natural ally of the petty bourgeoisie was deemed by the Kemalist leadership to be the Anatolian peasantry. It was in this group of independent small-holders in Central and Eastern Anatolia that the petty-bourgeois leadership hoped to find its mass base to defeat imperialism and suppress internal reaction cultivated by the Palace, the landlords, and the comprador bourgeoisie.

Although the peasants were first approached through the intermediary of sections of the rural petty bourgeoisie – primarily through local bureaucrats, army officers, and professional strata – the tradition-bound small-holding peasantry resisted any direct participation in or identification with the nationalist movement.[48] However contradictory an economic position the peasants held *vis-a-vis* the power and interests of the big landowners, their deep-seated religious beliefs led them to view their interests as corresponding more closely with those of the landlords and Islamic clergy than with an alien secularist national movement with which they had little or no basis of association in their day-to-day lives.

The numerous attempts by the Kemalist activists to enlist the peasants in the National Militia (*Kuvayi Milliye*) during the initial stages of the liberation struggle (1919–20) had resulted in failure. The peasants' distrust of and passive resistance against the Nationalist forces meant a heavy blow to the National Front in the early years of the Nationalist offensive. Despite difficulties, however, the Kemalists were able to strengthen the forces of the National Militia substantially, such that by mid-1920 there were 5,608 Nationalist guerrillas and 118 officers in the south of Izmir, and, together with those in the north and the Marmara region, their number totalled 15,000.[49] However, the Nationalist leadership was aware that, without the full support and participation of the Anatolian peasantry, they would lack the mass base essential for securing a Nationalist victory. It thus became clear that it was only through the intermediary of the landlords and the Islamic clergy that the Nationalist cadres would have any chance of enlisting the peasantry in the National Front.[50] This implied approaching forces that were hostile to the NLF and which had collaborated from the very beginning with both imperialism and the Ottoman Palace bureaucracy.

Placed in this contradictory position – of needing the support and participation of the peasant masses in the NLF on the one hand, and to achieve this the need to seek the assistance of collaborators of the imperialist enemy on the other – the Kemalist leadership had no other choice but to make concessions to the Anatolian *esraf* in order to secure their support, and through them the support and participation of the small-holding peasantry.[51]

The alliance between the Nationalist leadership and the *esraf* was first affirmed at the Erzurum Congress on July 23, 1919, and continued with the creation of the Grand National Assembly in Ankara on April 23, 1920. It was only after the consolidation of this alliance in the GNA that the National Front began to receive the gradual support of the Turkish peasantry.

State Power in Independent Turkey

Although the top leadership of the National Front always remained in the hands of petty-bourgeois military/civilian cadre and their direct support came largely from the urban and rural nationalist bureaucratic and professional strata, who were disproportionately represented within the Grand National Assembly, the presence, also, of large numbers of landlords, clergy and rural commercial elements as deputies in the Assembly prevented the petty bourgeoisie from achieving full control and consolidation of their rule in the First Assembly. Nevertheless, Kemal's tactical manoeuvre with the *esraf* in order to engage the peasantry on the side of the Nationalists against the main enemy paid off in the short run in securing a Nationalist victory.

The Sultanate was abolished subsequently in November 1922 and, shortly thereafter, the Ottoman Government met for the last time and dissolved itself. There was, however, a bitter struggle within the Assembly between the Kemalists and the *esraf* on the future of the Caliphate, with the Kemalists insisting on restriction of the Caliph's authority and the *esraf* demanding the strengthening and expansion of his powers. This internal factional struggle over the Caliphate led to the dissolution of the Grand National Assembly. The withdrawal of the landlord-clergy coalition from the Assembly, while weakening the bureaucrat-*esraf* alliance politically, did not affect in any real sense the process of national independence since the anti-imperialist struggle had already ended in victory well before the dissolution of the Grand National Assembly.

On April 16, 1923, the Assembly dissolved itself in preparation for new elections; and, in the meantime, M. Kemal, who had been struggling for an independent power base for the bureaucratic petty bourgeoisie, rallied his supporters around a new political party – the People's Party – which he began to form in December 1922.[52] It was largely through this party that the position of the petty-bourgeois bureaucrats was to improve further in the Second Assembly, which convened on August 11, 1923.[53] Through this organizational effort Kemal became elected overwhelmingly the first President of the Republic and consolidated the majority rule of the petty bourgeoisie within the Second Assembly. The initial phase of the post-colonial power struggle had thus come to an end as Turkey declared its political independence, as a Republic, at the end of October 1923. This marked the beginning of the reign of the petty-bourgeois military-civilian bureaucracy. Thus, the latter's control of state power was a clear sign of the movement toward the consolidation and institutionalization of bourgeois nationalism which was to open the way for independent, national capitalist development under the guidance and control of the state and the military-civilian bureaucracy.

References

1. K. Fisek, *Turkiye'de Kapitalizmin Gelismesi ve Isci Sinifi,* (The Development of Capitalism and the Working Class in Turkey), (Ankara: Dogan Yayinevi, 1969), pp. 9–35; O. C. Sarc, 'Ottoman Industrial Policy, 1840–1914', in C. Issawi (ed.), *The Economic History of the Middle East, 1800–1914: A Book of Readings,* (Chicago and London: University of Chicago Press, 1966), pp. 46–59; T. Cavdar (1970), *Osmanlilarin Yari-Somurge Olusu,* (The Semi-Colonization of the

Ottomans), (Istanbul: Ant Yayinlari, 1970).
2. O. Ozgur, (1976), *Sanayilesme ve Turkiye,* (Industrialization and Turkey), (Istanbul: Gercek Yayinevi, 1976), pp. 128–39; I. Cem, *Turkiye'de Geri Kalmisligin Tarihi,* (The History of Underdevelopment in Turkey), (Istanbul: Cem Yayinevi, 1974), pp. 148–250.
3. M. Akdag, *Celali Isyanlari,* (Celali Uprisings), (Ankara: Ankara Universitesi Basimevi, 1963); W. Griswold, 'Political Unrest and Rebellion in Anatolia, 1605–1609', (Unpublished Ph.D. thesis, University of California at Los Angeles, 1966); I. Cem, *op. cit.,* pp. 198–207.
4. B. Lewis, 'The Decline of the Ottoman Empire', in his *The Emergence of Modern Turkey,* 2nd edn., (London: Oxford University Press, 1969), pp. 36–9.
5. *Ibid.,* p. 37.
6. See the collection of essays in R. Hilton (ed.), *The Transition from Feudalism to Capitalism,* (London: New Left Books, 1976). Also see M. Dobb, *Studies in the Development of Capitalism,* (London: Routledge & Kegan Paul, 1963).
7. E.M. Earle, *Turkey, The Great Powers, and The Bagdad Railway: A Study in Imperialism,* (New York: Russell & Russell, 1966), p. 13; T. Cavdar, (1973), 'Cumhuriyet Devri Baslarken Turkiye Ekonomisi', (The Turkish Economy at the Beginning of the Republican Era), in *Turkiye Ekonomisinin 50 Yili Semineri,* (Seminar on the 50 Years of the Turkish Economy), (Bursa: I. ve T. I. Akademisi, 1973), p. 62.
8. O.C. Sarc, *op. cit.,* p. 49.
9. See Y.K. Tengirsenk, 'Tanzimat Devrinde Osmanli Devletinin Harici Ticaret Siyaseti', (The Ottoman Empire's Politics of External Trade During the Tanzimat Period), *Tanzimat I,* (Istanbul: Maarif Matbaasi, 1940), pp. 289–320; A. Yucekok, 'XIX. Yuzyil Osmanli Ticaret Sozlesmesi', (The 19th Century Ottoman Commercial Agreement), *Siyasal Bilgiler Fakultesi Dergisi,* (Journal of the Political Science Faculty), XXIII, 1 (1968), pp. 381–425. For the text of the Convention treaty, see Great Britain, *Parliamentary Papers,* 1839, L, pp. 291–95, (reproduced in C. Issawi (ed.), *op. cit.,* pp. 38–40).
10. F.E. Bailey, *British Policy and the Turkish Reform Movement,* (Cambridge, Mass.: Harvard University Press, 1942), Tables 8 and 14.
11. *Ibid.,* Tables 3, 5, 6, 7.
12. O.C. Sarc, *op. cit.,* pp. 49–50.
13. *Ibid.,* p. 51.
14. *Ibid.*
15. *Ibid.,* pp. 52–5.
16. A.D. Novichev, 'The Development of Agriculture in Anatolia', in C. Issawi (ed.), *op. cit.,* p. 67. A *donum* equals one-twelfth of a hectare or O. 206 acres.
17. *Ibid.,* p. 68.
18. However, this did not mean a complete blockage of capitalist development in Turkey, but a temporary halt in the development of a Turkish industrial bourgeoisie. The capitalism that did develop in the Empire from the 19th to the beginning of the 20th centuries was one of *dependent* capitalism, effected through the intermediary of the Ottoman

comprador bourgeoisie and having the support of the Palace bureaucracy.

19. R. Aktan, 'Agricultural Policy of Turkey', (unpublished Ph.D. dissertation, University of California, 1950), pp. 140–1, 162–73.
20. R.S. Suvla, 'Tanzimat Devrinde Istikrazlar', (Public Debts During the Tanzimat Period), in *Tanzimat*, (Istanbul, 1940), pp. 263–88.
21. Most of this debt was owed to two countries, with France accounting for 40% of all loans and England for 29% of the total in 1881. By 1914, however, the share of French creditors had increased to 49%, while that of the British had fallen to 7%, and that of Germany had risen to 20% – a four-fold increase since 1881. See State Institute of Statistics, *Turkiye'de Toplumsal ve Ekonomik Gelismenin 50 Yili,* (50 Years of Social and Economic Development in Turkey), (Ankara: S.I.S., 1973), pp. 17–19.
22. K. Fisek, 'Osmanli Dis Borclari Ustune', (On Ottoman External Debts), *Siyasal Bilgiler Fakultesi Dergisi,* XXII, 3 (1968).
23. D.C. Blaisdell, *European Financial Control in the Ottoman Empire,* (New York, 1929).
24. F. Ahmad, *The Young Turks: The Committee of Union and Progress in Turkish Politics, 1908–1914,* (London: Oxford University Press, 1969); B. Lewis, *op. cit.*, pp. 207–9; E.E. Ramsaur, *The Young Turks: Prelude to the Revolution of 1908,* (Beirut: Khayats, 1965).
25. Ahmad, *op. cit.*, Lewis, *op. cit.*, pp. 210–38.
26. *Ibid.*, pp. 207–8.
27. *Ibid.*, p. 209.
28. *Ibid.*, pp. 213–27.
29. N. Berkes, *The Development of Secularism in Turkey,* (Montreal: McGill University Press, 1964), p. 329.
30. By the end of the two Balkan Wars, the Ottomans had lost almost all of their European possessions to Bulgaria, Serbia, Greece, Montenegro and Albania. All in all, by mid-1913, the Ottomans had lost 83% of the territory and 69% of the population of their European provinces.
31. For a general discussion on the nature of the Asiatic mode of production, see: P. Anderson, 'The "Asiatic Mode of Production",' in *Lineages of the Absolutist State,* (London: New Left Books, 1974), pp. 462–549; H. Draper, 'Oriental Despotism' in *Karl Marx's Theory of Revolution,* (New York: Monthly Review Press, 1977), pp. 515–71; D.R. Gandy, *Marx and History,* (Austin and London: University of Texas Press, 1979), pp. 18–25; and L. Krader, *The Asiatic Mode of Production: Sources, Development and Critique in the Writings of Karl Marx,* (Assem: Van Gorkum & Co., 1975).

    With regard to the domination of the Asiatic mode in Ottoman Turkey, the following general observations are possible in terms of its origins and development. Following their invasion of the Byzantine Empire from Northeastern Anatolia in the 11th century, the Turkmen Oguz nomads from Central Asia came to occupy Eastern and Central Anatolia a century later. The ancestors of Osman, the founder of the dynasty, were members of the Kayi tribe who entered Anatolia along with these nomads. One of the independent Turkmen principalities established in Anatolia was that led by Osman. By 1300 Osman ruled an area stretching from Eskisehir to the plains of Iznik. And his successor

Orhan, by capturing Uskudar in 1338, had brought the growing Empire to the doorsteps of the Byzantine capital, Constantinople. From this point on, the Ottomans entered a long phase of territorial expansion in all directions.

Although it came into contact with numerous formations with different modes of production and exchange, Ottoman Turkey retained its dominant, despotic state for over seven centuries.

While private property in land and feudal relations of production began to develop in Ottoman Turkey in the 17th century and rapidly expanded and surpassed that owned by the state in many parts of the Empire by the 18th century, the feudal lords were never able to overthrow the central state and exert their own political domination over the Empire's affairs. Thus they continued to coexist with the developing Ottoman comprador bourgeoisie under the political rule of the dominant Asiatic state. State power remained in the hands of the despotic rulers and the Palace bureaucracy until the very end.

The transformation of the Ottoman Empire through the state structure did not take place until later, first by the Young Turks and subsequently by the Kemalist forces, representing the disaffected national and petty bourgeoisies. Their aim was to dismantle the Asiatic and feudal modes and in their place cultivate a local, national capitalism through the powers of the new state.

On the various aspects of the development process in Ottoman Turkey, especially with respect to the Asiatic mode, see S. Divitcioglu, *Asya Uretim Tarzi ve Osmanli Toplumu,* (The Asiatic Mode of Production and Ottoman Society), (Istanbul: Koz Yayinlari, 1971); O. Ozgur, (1976), *op. cit.,* pp. 100–32; H. Inalcik, (1964) 'The Nature of Traditional Society: Turkey', in R.E. Ward and D.A. Rustow (eds.), *Political Modernization in Japan and Turkey,* (Princeton: Princeton University Press, 1964), pp. 42–63; I. Cem, *op. cit.,* pp. 53–139; O. Kurmus, *Emperyalizmin Turkiye'ye Girisi,* (The Penetration of Imperialism into Turkey), (Istanbul: Bilim Yayinlari, 1974); T. Cavdar (1970), *op. cit.* For a critical view and attempted refutation of the Asiatic Mode thesis (stressing that Ottoman society was from the beginning a feudal society), see D. Avcioglu, *Turkiye'nin Duzeni,* (The Turkish Social Order), Vol. 1, (Istanbul: Tekin Yayinevi, 1975), pp. 13–31.

32. This was the allocation of parcels of conquered lands to *sipahis* (rural cavalry with military and administrative functions in the provinces) and to the civilian sector of the *devsirmes* (top officials of the central bureaucracy) in the form of fiefs (*timar*). The *sipahis* and civilian *devsirmes* were given these lands for the purpose of administering them in the name of the state. This system of land allocation was put into effect during the reign of Suleyman I. See H. Inalcik, (1973), *The Ottoman Empire,* (New York: Praeger Publishers, 1973), pp. 104–18; H. Islamoglu and S. Faroqhi, 'Crop Patterns and Agricultural Production Trends in Sixteenth-Century Anatolia', *Review,* II, 3 (Winter 1979), pp. 402–7 and 424–36; K. Fisek, *Turkiye'de Kapitalizmin Gelismesi ve Isci Sinifi, op. cit.,* pp. 21–2.

33. The *timar* system was in effect for quite some time. And as the central state began gradually to lose its authority in the countryside, the *sipahis*

and other fief holders increasingly evaded their obligations to the state and attempted to take over the ownership of state lands. Realizing that the old rural military/administrative system had outlived its usefulness, the state moved against the *sipahis* and displaced them. This was done, above all, by the introduction of tax-farming (*iltizam*). This process of transformation of the agrarian structure took place during the 17th and 18th centuries, and, as a result, a landed gentry (*ayan*) began to develop, displacing the *sipahis* as intermediaries between the state and the producers. Later, at the end of the 18th and the beginning of the 19th centuries, the *ayan* became a fully developed feudal landowning class and began to challenge the authority of the central state by equipping their own armies. Although they never became powerful enough to overthrow the political supremacy of the central state, they nonetheless came close to it: in 1893, Mehmet Ali Pasa, the strongest *ayan* of the time and the Governor of Egypt, defeated the Ottoman armies in Kutahya, not far from the Ottoman capital, Istanbul. Mehmet Ali's forces were soon driven back, however, by Britain and France, who intervened on behalf of the Ottoman throne. And Ali was only able to obtain recognition as hereditary ruler of Egypt. While the *ayans* were thus defeated in their bid for state power, they nevertheless continued to exercise economic control over vast areas of the Empire.

34. The following diagrams show the evolution of the different modes of production and exchange within the Ottoman formation from the 14th to the 20th centuries.

Figure 1
The Evolution of the Ottoman Empire, 1300–1920

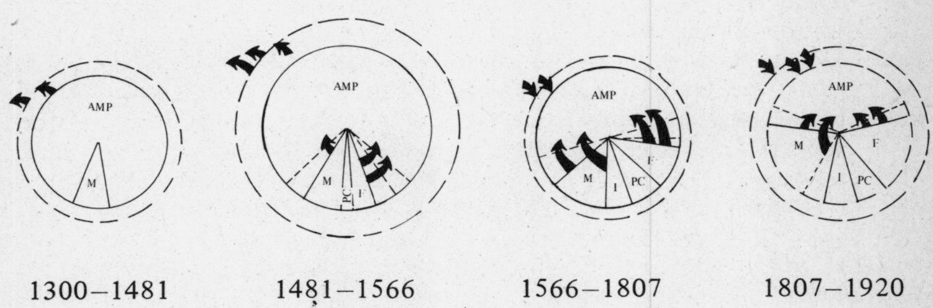

1300–1481 1481–1566 1566–1807 1807–1920

Legend:
AMP =Asiatic Mode of Production
F =Feudal forms of property based on non-wage labour
PC =Petty commodity production in town and country
M =Merchant capital
I =Industrial capital

35. N. Berkes, *op. cit.*, pp. 11–16; M. Sencer, *Osmanli Toplum Yapisi,* (The Ottoman Social Structure), (Istanbul: Ant Yayinlar, 1963); S. Divitcioglu, *op. cit.*, pp. 47–108.

36. D. Avcioglu, *op. cit.*, pp. 284–6; B. Lewis, *op. cit.*, pp. 454–6; H.A.R. Gibb and H. Bowen, *Islamic Society and the West*, Vol. I, (London: Oxford University Press, 1957).
37. The Izmir-Aydin and Istanbul-Baghdad railways are notable examples of this. As Rosa Luxemburg points out in her analysis of railway construction in Anatolian Turkey during this period, through this process not only did European capital gain access to vast resources of the Empire and extract surplus value from wage labour employed in railway construction, but even the financing of these projects was locally based and came directly from the Ottoman state treasury. See R. Luxemburg, *The Accumulation of Capital*, (New Haven: Yale University Press, 1951), pp. 439–445. Also see T. Cavdar, (1970), *op. cit.*, pp. 5–52, 110–67, and E.M. Earle. *op. cit.*
38. T. Cavdar, (1970), *op. cit.*; D. Ergil, (1975) 'From Empire to Dependence: The Evolution of Turkish Underdevelopment', (Unpublished Ph.D. dissertation, State University of New York at Binghamton, 1975), pp. 130–1.
39. 'National bourgeoisie' is defined here to signify that segment of the local capitalist class which owns and/or controls the means of industrial production. While the *comprador* bourgeoisie is mainly concentrated in import-export commerce and is directly tied to imperialism, the *national* bourgeoisie has an interest in safeguarding and protecting its property in the means of production (which is located within the confines of 'its own' national territory) from foreign rivals, with the objective of increased capital accumulation that would shift the bulk of locally generated profits from foreign (transnational) monopolies into their own accounts. It is this basic conflict between national and foreign capital that, objectively, sets the one against the other and leads the national bourgeoisie to join the national liberation struggle and adopt a nationalist and anti-imperialist stand within it.
40. As the following data show, the bulk of Ottoman industrial capital was in the hands of Greeks (50%) and Armenians (20%), with only 15% of the Empire's industrial capital under Turkish ownership.

Table 1
Distribution of Capital and Labour in Ottoman Industry by Nationality, 1915

Nationality	*Capital (%)*	*Labour (%)*
Turkish	15	15
Greek	50	60
Armenian	20	15
Jewish	5	10
Foreign	10	–
TOTAL	*100*	*100*

Source: State Institute of Statistics, *Turkiye'de Toplumsal ve Ekonomik Gelismenin 50 Yili*, p. 143.

41. *Ibid.*, p. 145. For a detailed analysis of the Turkish industrial proletariat during this period, see Y.N. Rozaliev, *Turkiye Sanayi Proletaryasi,* (The Turkish Industrial Proletariat), (Istanbul: Yar Yayinlari, 1974), pp. 17–25, 53–80.
42. As the above table shows, 60% of all those employed in Ottoman industry were Greeks, with 15% Armenians and 10% Jews; only 15% of Ottoman industrial workers were of Turkish national origin.
43. D. Ergil, (1975), *op. cit.*, p. 210.
44. O. Ozgur, (1972), *Turkiye'de Kapitalizmin Gelismesi,* (The Development of Capitalism in Turkey), (Istanbul: Gercek Yayinevi, 1972), pp. 79–81; I. Cem, *op. cit.*, pp. 310–11; D. Avcioglu, *op. cit.*, pp. 286–300.
45. Moreover, although landless peasants (or agricultural workers) constituted only 8% of farmer families, only a small number of peasants who did own land were able to survive without also working on the estates of the big landowners. D. Ergil and R. Rhodes, 'The Impact of the World Capitalist System on Ottoman Society', *Islamic Culture,* XLVIII, 2 (April 1974), p. 84.
46. 'Petty bourgeoisie' is defined here as those who own and/or control means of production, but employ no wage labourers. The self-employed (or small shopkeepers, artisans, and landed peasants) have traditionally been viewed as constituting the core of this class. The petty bourgeoisie is an intermediate class in that it is caught between the dominant ruling class(es) and the working class, with both of which it has certain shared characteristics. Like the big bourgeoisie and landlords, it owns or controls means of production, but, like the working class, it is directly engaged in the production process, hence it provides its own labour power. Thus, it is neither an exploiting class nor an exploited one. While the members of the petty bourgeoisie aspire to become big capitalists, their immediate interests centre around the safeguarding of their position as small, independent producers or merchants.
47. Largely made up of British, French, Italian, and Greek forces that had invaded and occupied different parts of Ottoman Turkey which required battle on several fronts simultaneously.
48. D. Avcioglu, *op. cit.*, pp. 280–4.
49. S. Selek, *Anadolu Ihtilali,* (Anatolian Revolution), (Istanbul, 1973), p. 125. According to Selek, the National Militia consisted of many diverse individuals, including bandits, military deserters, fugitive criminals, prisoners, thugs, impoverished and unemployed ex-peasants, as well as 'patriots' from various social classes – all unified under the common objective of liberating Turkey from imperialist occupation.
50. K. Steinhaus, *Ataturk Devrimi Sosyolojisi,* (The Sociology of the Ataturk Reforms), (Istanbul, 1970).
51. *Ibid.*
52. B. Lewis, *op. cit.*, p. 259.
53. The representation of petty-bourgeois bureaucrats (comprised of those drawn from the civil service, military, education, law, medicine, and other professions) substantially improved from the time of the Erzurum Congress, where they accounted for 57% of the delegates, to the First Assembly, where they constituted 63% of the deputies and to the Second Assembly, where they accounted for 78% of the deputies. The merchant-

landlord-clergy group fell from 43% to 35% to 20% of all deputies, respectively. S. Selek, *op. cit.*, p. 273, and F.W. Frey, *The Turkish Political Elite,* (Cambridge, Mass.: The M.I.T. Press, 1965), p. 181.

2. The Role of the State in National Economic Development in the 1920s

In this chapter our primary focus is on the Kemalist state and its role in national economic development in the period following Independence until the Great Depression at the close of the 1920s. Within this broader framework, our main interest is to examine the measures that were proposed and the policies that were adopted in the Grand National Assembly during the first six years of the Kemalist regime.

First, however, we shall briefly examine the level of development of the productive forces in Turkey at the time of Independence in the early 1920s, for it was the socio-economic conditions inherited from Ottoman society that the state had to confront in formulating its development policies after 1923.

The Level of Economic Development Inherited

Our earlier discussion of the social and class structure of Ottoman Turkey at the turn of the century described the prevailing relations of production in both the urban and rural settings throughout Anatolian Turkey during this period. In this section we present a brief outline of the level of development of the productive forces that corresponded to the prevailing relations of production in the Ottoman domain immediately before the Nationalist victory in the early 1920s.

The Agricultural Sector

The feudal agrarian structure, which was consolidated in rural Turkey under the *ayan, derebeys* and *agas* during the 19th century, remained intact until the mid-1920s and 1930s when the Kemalist regime launched and began to implement a nationwide agrarian reform.

Historically, a number of obstacles have hindered the development of agriculture in Ottoman Turkey. Firstly, the general poverty of the vast majority of the peasantry meant the availability of a large and cheap labour pool which the landlords could exploit; this minimized the introduction of new production techniques. Secondly, the rural tax system (*osur* or tithe) had an overburdening effect on the small-holding peasantry which prevented the expansion of and improvement in agricultural production at the middle and lower levels to any significant degree. Lastly the landlords' further role as usurer kept the peasants in perpetual debt-bondage with virtually little or no possibility for them ever to improve their lot, and so expand agricultural production.

As pointed out in the previous chapter, the Turkish countryside was characterized by a massive disparity in the ownership of land: a small number of rural families owned most of the arable land.[1] The mean size of holding for the top 1% of rural families was 300 hectares (or 741 acres), while 87% of rural families held an average of only 3.1 hectares (or 7.6 acres) of land. Because of the extremely small size of their holdings, many subsistence farmers became employed as part-time agricultural labourers in the service of large landlords.[2] This meant that, as long as there was a large number of peasants who needed more land, the *aga* received substantial returns as landlord (in the form of ground rent) and even larger returns as usurer. However,

> Neither the 'rent' nor the 'profit' from usury was usually or to any great extent converted into 'capital' for agricultural production . . . with the result that techniques of production remained primitive, volume varied as a simple function of the size of the peasantry (and within that according to weather conditions), and capital accumulation remained at a very low level or was non-existent.[3]

The second major obstacle contributing to the impoverishment of the Turkish peasantry and, with it, the impoverishment and backwardness of Turkish agriculture, was the heavy burden of the rural tax on production. This fell largely on the middle and small-holding peasantry. This tax system (*osur*) was one of the main mechanisms underpinning the landlord-usurer's (*aga's*) sovereignty and the peasant's dependence within the prevailing socio-economic structure of rural Turkey:

> The *osur* or tithe, which every peasant had to pay . . . [was collected] by each peasant's tax farmer or landlord, and it was paid in kind, not cash. Initially fixed at one-tenth of the annual produce, *osur* was increased as the State's need for revenue increased, reaching one-eighth and even at one time one-fifth . . . *Osur* was a tax on production, not on income, and so it basically took from the peasantry such 'surplus' as their own subsistence needs and the payments to the *agas* permitted. It thus took, in effect, that part of the produce which could otherwise have been marketed by the peasants and the resulting cash proceeds which could have been converted by them into 'capital'. As it was, no, or very little, capital accumulation took place in the hands of the cultivators until the abolition of the tithe in 1925.[4]

The third major factor that contributed to the persistent backwardness of Turkish agriculture was the lifelong indebtedness of the peasant producers to the local landlords, and the high interest that such loans entailed. In addition to their ownership of large tracts of land (on which the surplus product was appropriated by the landlords, through the exploitation of landless agricultural labourers and peasant share-croppers) *and* their pocketing of a part of the *osur*, which they collected for the state, the landlord-usurers also collected interest on loans advanced to the peasants. Through the mechanism of debt-bondage, this ensured the perpetual subordination of peasants for as long as the landlords remained the dominant class throughout rural Turkey. The debt relationship which developed between the *agas* and the peasants was a permanent feature of the rural socio-economic structure under which the impoverished peasants became totally dependent on the *agas* for credit and cash to survive.

Given this rural structure in which the landlords became wealthy so easily, there were no compelling reasons for them to modernize the tools and techniques of production. Consequently, and in the absence of any significant foreign investment in the agrarian sector, the level of development of the productive forces remained very low and stagnated for decades. This backward agricultural sector, however, played a predominant role in the Ottoman economy, accounting for 54% of the Gross National Product (GNP) in the period immediately preceding World War I (see Table 2).

Table 2
Sectoral Composition of Gross National Product, 1914

Sector	*Size (million O.L.)**	*Percentage*
Agriculture	13,060	54
Mining	105	—
Manufacturing Industry	2,443	10
Commerce	1,832	8
Government Services	1,878	8
Free Professions and Services	1,130	5
Construction	442	2
All Other Sectors	3,217	13
Total Gross National Product	24,107	100

* In current prices (Ottoman Lira).
Source: State Institute of Statistics, *Turkiye'de Toplumsal ve Ekonomik Gelismenin 50 Yili*, (Ankara: Devlet Istatistik Enstitusu Matbaasi, 1973), p. 21.

Notwithstanding the significant contribution of the agrarian sector to the Ottoman economy, the archaic feudal structures of social and economic backwardness in Ottoman Turkey perpetuated the polarization of the Turkish

countryside into big estates and small subsistence plots – an agrarian structure that persisted and remained essentially unchallenged for decades, until the rise to leadership of Kemalist forces and the latter's consolidation of state power in the 1920s.

The Industrial Sector

In contrast to agriculture, the contribution of Ottoman industry to the GNP was minimal (10% in 1914) and most of it was generated by enterprises owned and controlled by foreign capital[5] and the minority bourgeoisie.

The distribution of capital in Ottoman industry was highly concentrated in the hands of the minority bourgeoisie (50% of all industrial capital was held by Greeks alone), leaving only 15% in the hands of Turkish industrialists. Moreover, the small-scale light manufacturing enterprises owned by the minority bourgeoisie were more an extension of the latter's position as a comprador class than that initiated by a full-fledged industrial bourgeoisie. Thus, the development of local industry remained subservient to the changing *commercial* interests of the minority bourgeoisie *vis-a-vis* the European metropolis, and what expansion did take place in Ottoman industry was largely through state support and in branches of industry that would not compete with their import activities. The most numerous manufacturing operations were those processing primary products (cotton, leather, lumber) for export. Textiles, which in 1915 accounted for 27.6% of the industrial enterprises, still provided only 25% of the Empire's needs; the rest had to be imported.[6] Hence, light manufacturing was developed in accordance with the import-export activities of the minority comprador bourgeoisie. Consequently, Ottoman industry experienced little growth – the economy growing at no more than 1% annually during the two decades preceding the final collapse of the Empire.[7] Moreover, the limited industrialization that did take place was concentrated largely in two port cities, Istanbul (with 55% of all industrial enterprises) and Izmir (with 22%).[8]

Foreign capital during this period was largely concentrated in the construction and operation of railways, with the aim of securing access to the oil and mineral-rich areas of the Empire. Of the 5,711 million Ottoman *kurus* invested in Turkey by foreign capital up to World War I, 3,368 million *kurus* (or 59%) was in railway construction.[9] Of all the various railway concessions to European capitalists, the most important was the Baghdad Railway Concession of 1903 to the *Deutsche Bank* of Berlin.[10] The importance of the construction of the Baghdad Railway to European (mainly German) capital lay not in its transportation or communication value *per se*, but in its role as a vehicle of penetration into the Empire's resource-rich regions of Anatolia and Mesopotamia. These areas, as E.M. Earle points out,

> possessed vast resources of some of the most essential materials of modern industry: minerals, fuel, lubricants, abrasives. Its deposits of oil alone were enough to arouse the cupidity of the Great Powers . . . [It] was anticipated that the Ottoman Empire would prove a valuable

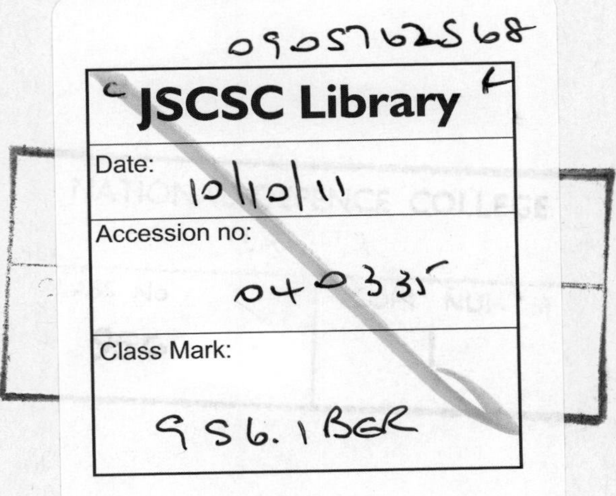

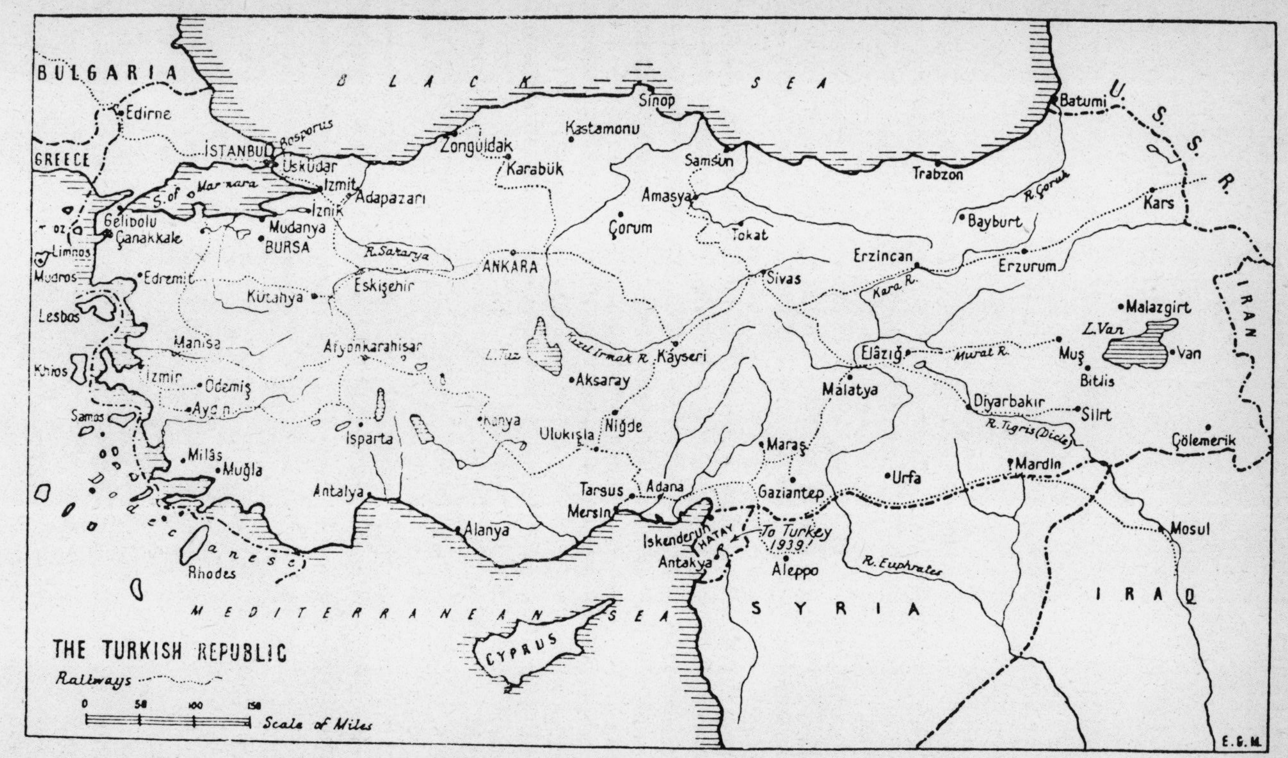
BULGARIA
GREECE
BLACK SEA
U.S.S.R.
IRAN
IRAQ
SYRIA
MEDITERRANEAN SEA
CYPRUS
Edirne
İSTANBUL
Bosporus
Üsküdar
S. of Marmara
İzmit
Adapazarı
İznik
Mudanya
BURSA
Gelibolu
Çanakkale
Limnos
Mudros
Lesbos
Khios
Samos
Dodecanese
Rhodes
Edremit
Manisa
İzmir
Ödemiş
Milâs
Muğla
Kütahya
Eskişehir
R. Sakarya
Afyonkarahisar
Isparta
Antalya
Alanya
Zonguldak
Karabük
Kastamonu
Sinop
ANKARA
L. Tuz
Konya
Ulukışla
Aksaray
Niğde
Kızıl Irmak R.
Kayseri
Çorum
Amasya
Samsun
Tokat
Sivas
Tarsus
Adana
Mersin
Iskenderun
HATAY
To Turkey 1939
Antakya
Aleppo
Gaziantep
Maraş
Malatya
Elâzığ
Urfa
Erzincan
Kara R.
Trabzon
Bayburt
R. Çoruh
Erzurum
Batumi
Kars
Malazgirt
L. Van
Van
Muş
Murat R.
Bitlis
Diyarbakır
Siirt
R. Tigris (Dicle)
Mardin
Çölemerik
Mosul
R. Euphrates
THE TURKISH REPUBLIC
Railways
0
50
100
150
Scale of Miles
E.G.M.

> source of essential raw materials, a satisfactory market for finished products, and a rich field for the investment of capital. Economically, the territory served by the Baghdad Railway was one of the most important undeveloped regions of the world.[11]

Building on its earlier foothold in the Empire's economy, acquired through previous concessions for railway construction in the late 1880s which had already effected sharp increases in Ottoman-German trade by 1893,[12] Germany was, by the turn of the century, beginning to break the monopoly held by France and Britain over Ottoman finance and trade. This Baghdad Railway Concession, coupled with these earlier developments, was later to assure the predominance of German capital over its capitalist rivals in controlling large portions of the Ottoman economy. Thus, in 1904, shortly after the approval of the Concession, 'the *Deutsche Bank,* of Berlin, promoters of the Baghdad Railway, obtained the privilege of making a thorough survey of the oilfields of the Tigris and Euphrates valleys, with the option within one year of entering into a contract with the Ottoman Government for their exploitation'.[13]

While German capital was beginning to consolidate its position in Turkey during the first decade of this century, the United States was in the process of full-scale entry into the world economy. The declining Ottoman Empire, with its enormous oil and other natural resources, proved to be a fertile ground for extending US corporate interests into the Middle East. American influence over the Turkish economy began with a rapid increase in the volume of trade between the two countries. Thus, while at the opening of the 20th century the volume of U.S. exports to Turkey amounted to US$50,000, by 1913 it had risen to US$3,500,000 and by 1920 to US$42,200,000.[14] And in the case of US imports from Turkey, the volume had risen from US$22,100,000 in 1913 to US$39,600,000 in 1920.[15] This expansion in trade was followed by numerous investments in key branches of the Turkish economy after the end of World War I. The most important of these was helped by Admiral Colby M. Chester, of the United States Navy, who negotiated with the Nationalist Government in Ankara new concessions for railway construction that were to result in the development of the oil industry in the Asiatic provinces of Turkey.[16] The entry of the United States into the Turkish economy led to another round of inter-imperialist rivalry over the Empire's vast resources situated in its rapidly contracting but still substantial territory.

Given the predominance of foreign capital in Ottoman industry for decades, industrial development in Turkey was mainly relegated to those areas of the economy that directly benefited foreign capital – i.e. raw materials and mineral extraction, and transport systems connected with their export. Under these conditions, coupled with the adverse effects of external control over Ottoman foreign trade, local industry was not able to grow as did its metropolitan counterparts during this period. Consequently, the level of development of the productive forces remained low in the industrial sector, much as in agriculture, and stagnated for decades until the Kemalist forces assumed state power in the early 1920s.

Economic Policies of the New Kemalist State

The Izmir Economic Congress, which convened from February 17 to March 4, 1923, marks the beginning of the active role of the new Kemalist state in the formulation of economic policy – a policy which was to guide the post-independence economic development of Turkey along a capitalist path.[17] Although the 1,135 delegates in the Congress were said to be representing a broad spectrum of diverse class forces, the Congress was carefully controlled and directed by the Turkish compradors of Istanbul and the big landowners of Anatolia. The main aim of the merchant class of Istanbul, which had organized into the *Milli Turk Ticaret Birligi* (Turkish National Commercial Association), was to take over the business of the minority bourgeoisie and to expand its own commercial base to maintain a competitive position *vis-a-vis* metropolitan firms. The heavy representation of Turkish compradors in the Izmir Congress, and the virtual absence of opposition to their demands there, led the state to grant them numerous concessions in the hope that this class would eventually merge with existing, small and fragmented local manufacturing groups and develop into a full-fledged national industrial bourgeoisie. The presence also of considerable numbers of large landowners at the Congress, and their open collaboration with other dominant classes represented there, was instrumental in suppressing the interests of workers and peasants and in safeguarding their firm hold over the land, blocking any attempts to open the question of land reform.[18]

The Izmir Economic Congress ended with the reaffirmation by the state of its commitment to protect the national capitalist class from the metropolitan bourgeoisie and to reconcile the diverse interests of the dominant national classes, in order to rally them behind its programme to 'modernize' and 'develop' the Turkish economy along capitalist lines.

State intervention in favour of local capitalists accelerated throughout the late 1920s in line with the Kemalist leadership's hope of building up the economic base of the nation through state encouragement of capital accumulation by the local bourgeoisie.

The Role of the State in Encouraging Turkish Industry

In the absence of a thorough internal social transformation that would alter substantially existing relations of production, the modified form of capitalist accumulation – now controlled and directed by the state – continued to be subjected to the laws of motion of the capitalist mode of production. Now, however, it was the state which undertook many of the tasks traditionally assumed elsewhere by the national industrial bourgeoisie. The state's role in the economy began to expand as it entered various branches of local industry to develop the infrastructure, establish banks, and regulate commerce – all co-ordinated within the broader framework of the national economy.

Among the most notable activities of the state in the spheres of industrial production and finance/credit were the development and expansion of state-owned and controlled enterprises in sugar, glass, leather, cotton yarn, woollen textiles, and the cement industry, and the establishment of several major industrial and commercial banks.[19]

One of the most important financial projects undertaken during this period was the establishment in 1924 of the *Is Bankasi* (Business Bank). Although founded as a private bank by Celal Bayar, who was asked to resign from his post as Minister of Development to become President of the Bank, its funds were provided mainly by top state officials and their associates. The Business Bank thus became one of the very first state-promoted 'private' enterprises set up as a model for future capitalist development in Turkey.[20] Indeed, the Bank was instrumental in encouraging the expansion of native industry and played a key role in the financing of many businesses, like the Alpullu Sugar Plant and the Pasabahce Glass and Bottle Factory.

In line with its development programme, the state also established two government-owned banks, *Sanayi ve Maadin Bankasi* (The Industrial and Mineral Bank) and *Ziraat Bankasi* (The Agricultural Bank), to expand capital accumulation in the hands of Turkish industrialists in the cities and to transform the countryside into modern, mechanized, productive agriculture. Between 1925 and 1932, the Industrial and Mineral Bank participated directly in more than a dozen privately owned firms with an initial capital of 1,173,000 Turkish lira (T.L.), and it also extended credits amounting to a total of 3.8 million T.L. to newly established private firms.[21] At the same time, this bank was also quite successful in aiding the expansion and profitability of a number of textile factories in Istanbul, where in return for an investment of 4,089,000 T.L. in four state-owned enterprises, it made a net profit of 3,877,000 T.L. in the course of a few years.[22] And, as a result of the modernization and expansion of these plants, the value of these four factories increased from 2,914,000 T.L. in the late 1920s to 8,512,000 T.L. in early 1933.[23] As for the government owned agricultural bank, *Ziraat Bankasi,* it extended substantial credits to big landowners in Central and Southern Turkey in the hope of transforming the countryside from a backward, stagnant economy to a modern, capitalist one. The volume of agricultural credits extended by the bank totalled 17 million T.L. in 1924; and by 1930 it had reached 36 million.[24]

In addition to the direct role played by various state banks and credit institutions in encouraging the expansion of national industry, many special laws were passed by the Grand National Assembly granting major concessions to private capital. The sugar industry provides one of the best examples of the nature and scope of the concessions granted to private capital during this period.

The first sugar factory was built in Alpullu, Thrace, with such extraordinary concessions as a 25-year monopoly in the five provinces in the vicinity, exemption from the Consumption Tax for 18 years, exemption from the Land Tax for 10 years on the lands on which the beets were grown for the factory, free construction land for the factory up to five hectares, exemption of the factory personnel from the payment of Income Tax for 10 years, etc. The entrepreneurs of the Alpullu sugar enterprise included deputies in the GNA [Grand National Assembly] and Istanbul merchants, who influenced the IB [Business Bank] into providing 68% of the capital and the ZB [Agricultural Bank] 10%, leaving only 22% to be supplied by themselves. Thus, the first and major sugar industry in Turkey was created by state funds for the profit of private interests.[25]

The advantages granted to other branches of Turkish industry were quite similar. For example, the Pasabahce Glass and Bottle Factory – one of the most profitable enterprises in Turkey – was 99% financed by the Business Bank, and was also granted a 25-year monopoly in eight provinces. And, as in the case of the textile industry, the state acquired full ownership and control of petroleum, explosives, paper, salt and, later, cement industries, the railways, major seaport facilities in Istanbul, Izmir, Trabzon and Mersin, and a number of enterprises in mining and extractive industries, to name only a few. But the state's extensive participation in, and control of, the national industrial economy was not to come to full bloom until the mid-1930s. For the moment its task was primarily to *encourage – not* to take over – private industry. This was made clear by Celal Bayar, the founder of the Business Bank (and later the Third President of the Republic between 1950 and 1960), who stated quite plainly in his address to local industrialists at the opening ceremony of the new Nazilli Textile Factory:

We will establish here a large textile factory. Since your capital is insufficient, the state will assume this task. And after you accumulate enough capital through state aid, we will gradually transfer the ownership of state enterprises in this field over to you.[26]

Important legislation to encourage industrialization through private capital during this period came with the passage of the Law for the Encouragement of Industry on May 28, 1927.

The Law divided the enterprises into four categories, from the largest which would enjoy all the benefits of the Law down to artisan shops. Mines were also covered, with the exception of quarries. The encouragement of even the smallest 'industrial shops' meant the support not only of the big bourgeoisie but also of the petty bourgeoisie. All of which was consistent with the corporatist leanings of the new regime, which in principle did not favour one class against the other, but in practice channelled most of the benefits proclaimed by the Law to the largest firms.[27]

The main advantages provided by the Law can be summarized as follows:[28] (1) Land grants up to 10 hectares would be free, and if necessary land would be expropriated for this purpose by a special law or purchased from public authorities such as municipalities; (2) the buildings and premises and all other installations of these enterprises would be exempt from such taxes as the immovable property tax, the land tax, the profit tax, and surcharges on all previous taxes due to provinces and municipalities; (3) materials needed for the construction of an enterprise and machinery needed for its operation would be exempt from customs dues and be granted a reduction of 30% on railway transport and shipping charges (this reduction could also be applied to other products and raw materials by special government decree); (4) the government could, upon request of the Ministry of Economics, issue permits for certain enterprises to buy the products of state monopolies at reduced rates or grant premiums (in the form of tax rebates or higher prices); (5) industrial enterprises would be granted a subsidy (investment fund) of up to 10% of the value of annual production; (6) industrial enterprises would be exempt from telegraph and telephone installation costs and operating charges; (7) bonds and securities of companies established for industrial purposes would be free from stamp duties; (8) entrepreneurs who established an entirely new industry would be given monopoly privileges for 25 years; (9) the approved firms could claim bonuses or price reductions in purchases from state factories.

Despite these extraordinary advantages provided by the state to private capital, the Turkish bourgeoisie lagged far behind the state's expectations of rapid industrialization. The reasons for the failure of the initial phase of the industrialization process in the 1920s are varied and complex and will be examined later in this chapter. But suffice it to say that with the increase in the number of enterprises supported by the state – from 470 in 1927 to 1,473 in 1933[29] – the state began to assume an even greater role in and more complete control over the national economy at the end of the 1920s and during the 1930s, as will be seen in Chapter Three.

The Role of the State in the Agrarian Sector

Parallel to the process of development and expansion of native industry, a number of important steps were also taken by the state in this period to accelerate the process of capital accumulation in the countryside. Among these were the abolition of the *osur* (tithe tax) in 1925 and the distribution of land to landless peasants through laws passed in 1927 and 1929.[30] As a result, by 1934 a total of 7,114,315 *donum* (or 17,785,787 acres) of land had been distributed to those without land.[31] However, all this land was state-owned public land, as the state was as yet reluctant to confront the powerful landlords by expropriating 'their' land.

Although a thorough transformation of the agrarian structure was not carried out during these initial years, the state

> did, however, attempt to increase production by establishing experimental stations, agricultural schools, and modern demonstration (state-owned) farms. Improved seed was provided and instructors were sent to villages to show new ways of cultivation. Compulsory agricultural training was instituted for soldiers during their military service. This 'productionist', rather than 're-distributionist', strategy led the Turkish Government to adopt two new programmes: encouragement of mechanization in agriculture and establishment of credit and marketing cooperatives.[32]

Thus, the state was primarily interested in increasing production to generate a large agricultural surplus and thereby to improve the country's position in exports. The Kemalists thought that the introduction of capitalist methods in agriculture would – with state aid in the supply of credit, means of production, and distribution – increase efficiency, productivity and the accumulation of capital in the countryside, a process that would parallel and supplement developments in the urban industrial sector.

However, because existing relations of production were kept intact in the countryside, and the economic, political, and socio-religious strength of the *esraf* and their domination over local branches of the state initiated Credit Unions and Producer Co-operatives continued alongside their representation in the Grand National Assembly, the financial resources of the co-operatives and the credits granted through the state owned Agricultural Bank were all diverted to their own private accounts. Thus, while in this way the landlords were able to expand their fortunes and further enrich themselves, landless peasants and small producers continued to be enslaved to them as in the past.

The landlords' control over the mechanism of state aid to the agricultural sector did, nevertheless, expand the growth of output in some sectors of the rural economy. And while this growth was sufficient to divert the state's attention to other areas of the national economy, the increased revenues accruing to the landlords further strengthened their material position in relation to other propertied classes such that the possibility of a genuine agrarian reform was to become very remote after the 1920s.

Obstacles to National Industrialization

Despite the extensive efforts of the state to aid the development of Turkish industry and agriculture during the 1920s, capitalist development failed to achieve the results envisaged by the state in trying to elevate Turkey to a full-fledged capitalist nation with a competitive edge in the world market for industrial goods. There were numerous obstacles to the industrialization of the country during this period and, of these, three were decisive: (1) the resistance of landlords in areas where their interests were threatened by industrial expansion; (2) the failure of the expected transformation of Turkish compradors into industrial capitalists; and (3) the unfavourable terms of the Treaty of Lausanne, in force from 1925 until 1929.

Internal reaction, led by the landlord-clergy coalition, viewed the industrialization efforts of the state as part of the process of modernization which challenged their control over the countryside. Resistance against these efforts succeeded in blocking the expansion of indigenous industry into the rural interior, leaving the control over vast sections of Anatolia exclusively in the hands of big landowners and the *esraf.* As a result, the limited transformation that did take place in the agrarian sector was almost exclusively in the sphere of agricultural production and this did not alter the conditions prevailing there in favour of industrialization.

The second major obstacle to the growth and expansion of local industry was the reluctance of the comprador bourgeoisie to expand into the industrial sector which the state consistently encouraged through credit, grants and numerous important concessions. Rather than employ the loans, credits, supplies, etc. provided by the state to expand production, most of them simply failed to take advantage of these concessions. Instead –

> the majority of the so-called entrepreneurs initiated 'paper' businesses, claimed the bonuses offered by the government, bought the products of the state factories well under their market prices, and sold them to other operators. After making exorbitant profits, they closed their 'enterprises' before they even started them. Even heavy machinery imported for the establishment of new industries was exported to other countries after their registration at Turkish ports of entry.[33]

Thus the profits made by the big merchants were generally employed in usury and commerce, not industrial production.

The third major obstacle to the development of industry was Turkey's adherence to the provisions of the Treaty of Lausanne for a period of five years (1924–1929) during which the country continued to recognize the economic concessions granted to foreign firms by the Ottoman Empire prior to 1914. Moreover, it was further agreed that Turkey would keep her customs duties to the level specified by the Ottoman customs tariff of September 1, 1916.[34] So the state was unable, until 1929, to develop a customs policy that would offset Turkey's trade deficit. The lack of significant revenues from customs, because of the restrictions in the Treaty, coupled with the abolition of the *osur* (rural tax on production) in 1925 (which at that time constituted 28.6% of public revenues), also worked against the full-scale participation of the state in the industrialization process during this period. The expiration of the Treaty in 1929 thus marks an important turning point for increased state intervention in the Turkish economy.

Although serious efforts were made by the Nationalist leadership to accelerate industrialization by providing domestic finance and a guarded acceptance of foreign capital in various branches of the national economy, Turkey remained a part of the metropolitan-controlled capitalist world economy until the end of the 1920s. Turkey's continued role as a supplier of raw materials and agricultural products and an importer of finished manufactured goods was determined by forces at work at the global level, forces which subjected Turkey to the dynamics of development at the centre of the world capitalist economy. It is for this reason that the metropolitan depression of 1929–30 had an immense impact on the Turkish economy.

The financial collapse in the metropolitan countries in 1929, lasting until at least the mid-1930s, affected the Turkish economy largely through external trade. The severance of commercial ties between Turkey and the metropolitan countries not only meant a major cut in the supply of manufactured goods to Turkey, but also a drastic drop in foreign demand for Turkey's exports of raw materials and agricultural produce – her largest categories of exports. The resulting drop in the value of the Turkish Lira led to a major decline in the prices of agricultural products,[35] affecting the balance of trade, agricultural revenues and, ultimately, the State Treasury. With the coming of the Depression, then, Turkey began to experience considerable difficulty in finding foreign markets for her agricultural produce and other primary products and thus lacked the foreign exchange necessary to continue importing capital equipment essential for the industrialization process. The drastic fall in Turkish export earnings and value of imports during the early years of the Depression (see Table 3) made industrialization through dependence on metropolitan economies virtually impossible.[36]

Table 3
Turkish Foreign Trade, 1929–33 (in millions of Turkish Lira)

Year	*Imports*	*Exports*
1929	256.0	155.0
1930	147.5	151.5
1931	126.7	127.3
1932	86.0	101.3
1933	74.6	96.2

Sources: Istatistik Umum Mudurlugu, *Aylik Istatistik Bulteni,* (Ankara: I.U.M., May 1956, June 1958); United Nations Statistical Office, *Yearbook of International Trade Statistics, 1950,* (New York: United Nations, 1951), Table 1, p. 149.

The wide-ranging expansion of the State into all branches of the national economy during the 1930s was in large measure a direct response to the adverse conditions created by the financial collapse in the metropolitan countries. These developments, coupled with the fact that the Depression in the West had not affected the structure of the Soviet economy (where, on the contrary, a major expansion was underway with the inauguration of the First Five Year Plan in 1928), were enough to convince the Kemalist bureaucracy to take decisive steps in moving the state to the forefront of the national economy, assuming more forcefully the role of entrepreneur, taking on many of the tasks traditionally performed by the national industrial bourgeoisie. With the state beginning to assume the commanding heights of the economy in the early 1930s, Turkey thus entered a unique period of capitalist development which was later to be called '*devletcilik*' or 'statism', and which marked the beginning of the period of consolidation of state capitalism in post-independence Turkey.

References

1. See pp. 6 and 8 above for data on the distribution of land ownership in Ottoman Turkey in 1913.
2. I. Husrev, *Turkiye Koy Iktisadiyati,* pp. 134–42.
3. D. Ergil, (1975), 'From Empire to Dependence', pp. 198–99.
4. *Ibid.*
5. In 1914, out of a total of 244 industrial enterprises in the Ottoman Empire, 190 were foreign owned. See U. Trumpener, *Germany and the Ottoman Empire, 1914–1918,* (Princeton: Princeton University Press, 1968), p. 9.
6. T. Cavdar, (1973), 'Cumhuriyet Donemi Baslarken . . .', p. 161.
7. V. Eldem, *Osmanli Imparatorlugu'nun Iktisadi Sartlari Hakkinda Bir Tetkik,* (An Examination of the Economic Condition of the Ottoman Empire), (Ankara, 1970), p. 308ff.
8. *Ibid.* For an official accounting of the number of factories in Istanbul and Izmir in 1915 by various branches of industry, see United States Department of Commerce, *Turkey: A Commercial and Industrial Handbook,* (Compiled by G. Bie Ravndal, American Consul General, Constantinople), (Washington: Government Printing Office, 1926), pp. 160–1.
9. Only 11% of all foreign investment was in manufacturing industry, with 10% in finance and insurance, 6% in mining, 5% each in public works and port facilities, and 4% in trade. State Institute of Statistics, *Turkiye'de Toplumsal ve Ekonomik Gelismenin 50 Yili,* p. 19.
10. This was a concession for 99 years for the building of a railway line from Konya to Baghdad, via Mosul. The entire project, with branch lines reaching to the Persian Gulf, provided for a total of almost 2,400 miles of railway. H.N. Howard, *The Partition of Turkey,* (New York: Howard Hertig, 1966), p. 48.
11. E.M. Earle, *Turkey, The Great Powers, and The Baghdad Railway: A Study in Imperialism,* p. 5. Earle goes on to point out that Anatolia 'is a great storehouse of important metals. A fine quality of chrome ore is to be found in the region directly south of the Sea of Marmara and in Cilicia . . . There are valuable deposits of antimony in the *vilayets* of Bursa and Smyrna, as well as commercially profitable lead and zinc mines near Bursa, Ismid, and Konia . . . In the vicinity of Diarbekir

there are mines which . . . promise to yield large supplies of copper . . . Boracite, mercury, nickel, iron, manganese, sulphur, and other minerals are to be found in Anatolia . . . [whose] coal deposits are not inconsiderable . . . In addition to coal, Anatolia possesses large deposits of lignite which, mixed with coal, is suitable fuel for ships, locomotives, gasworks, and factories. Oil exists in large quantities in Mesopotamia . . . Here in the Near East, then, was a great empire awaiting exploitation by Western capital and Western technical skill'. *Ibid.*, pp. 13–17.

12. In 1888, the year marking the first railway concession to the *Deutsche Bank*, German exports to Turkey were valued at 11,700,000 marks; by 1893, when the line was completed to Ankara by the German-owned Anatolian Railway Company, they had risen to a value of 40,900,000 marks, an increase of about 350%. German imports from Turkey during this same period rose from 2,300,000 marks to 16,500,000 marks, an increase of over 70%. *Ibid.*, p. 36.
13. *Ibid.*, p. 15. Three years earlier, in 1901, a German technical commission had already issued a favourable report on Mesopotamian petroleum resources, stating that 'the region was a veritable "lake of petroleum" of almost inexhaustible supply'. *Ibid.*
14. *Ibid.*, p. 339.
15. *Ibid.*
16. The American promoters of the Chester Lines were 'granted exclusive rights to the exploitation of all mineral resources, including oil, lying within a zone of twenty kilometres on each side of the railway lines'. *Ibid.*, p. 341.
17. See O. Ozgur, (1976), *Sanayilesme ve Turkiye*, pp. 154–62; K. Boratav, *Turkiye'de Devletcilik*, (Statism in Turkey), (Istanbul: Gercek Yayinevi, 1974), pp. 17–31; A.G. Okcun, *Turkiye Iktisat Kongresi*, (Turkish Economic Congress), (Ankara, 1971); A.H. Basar, '1923 Turkiye Iktisat Kongresinden 1948 Turkiye Iktisat Kongresine', (From the Turkish Economic Congress of 1923 to the Turkish Economic Congress of 1948), *Turkiye Iktisat Mecmuasi*, (Turkish Economic Review), No. 10, (November 1948); H. Derin, *Turkiye'de Devletcilik*, (Statism in Turkey), (Istanbul, 1940); D. Avcioglu, *Turkiye'nin Duzeni*, pp. 340–51.
18. D. Avcioglu, *ibid.*, pp. 354–6. The lack of direct representation for the Anatolian peasantry (there was merely the intermediary of big landlords who were classified as '*ciftci*' or 'farmers'!) and the absence of working-class representation through independent workers' organizations (instead, the worker-delegates were selected by the Turkish National Commercial Association from some groups of workers it had recently organized) effectively prevented the labouring masses from raising genuine demands for the improvement of their condition. See O. Ozgur, (1976), *op. cit.*, pp. 158–9. Also see A.H. Basar, *Baris Dunyasi*, No. 54, and A.G. Okcun, *op. cit.*, pp.430–7.
19. Z.Y. Hershlag, *Turkey: The Challenge of Growth*, (Leiden: E.J. Brill, 1968), pp. 47–58; K. Boratav, *op. cit.*, pp. 31–40; D. Avcioglu, *op. cit.*, pp. 367–416; O. Ozgur; (1976), *op. cit.*, pp. 162–8; 162–8; K. Fisek, *Turkiye'de Kapitalizmin Gelismesi ve Isci Sinifi*, pp. 57–63.
20. O. Ozgur, (1976), *op. cit.*, pp. 164–5.
21. D. Avcioglu, *op. cit.*, p. 380.

22. *Ibid.*, p. 381.
23. *Ibid.*
24. O. Ozgur, (1976), *op. cit.*, p. 163.
25. D. Ergil, (1975), *op. cit.*, p. 352. And, as D. Avcioglu points out, later on two more sugar factories – one at Eskisehir and another at Turhal – were established through the initiative of the Business Bank (which supplied 51% of the capital) and the Agricultural Bank (which contributed 49%). D Avcioglu, *op. cit.*, p. 384.
26. Celal Bayar, quoted in O. Ozgur, (1976), *op. cit.*, p. 168 (my translation).
27. D. Ergil, (1975), *op. cit.*, p. 354.
28. Loi sur l'Encouragement de l'Industrie, Loi No. 1055 de Mai 1927, printed in *Journal Officiel,* No. 608, du 15 Juin 1927, as summarized in *ibid.*, pp. 354–5.
29. H. Derin, *op. cit.*, p. 83.
30. S. Aksoy, *Turkiye'de Toprak Meselesi,* (The Land Question in Turkey), (Istanbul: Gercek Yayinevi, 1971), pp. 52–67.
31. *Ibid.*, p. 58. Among those receiving land were newly arrived immigrants from the old Ottoman provinces in the Balkans.
32. D. Ergil, (1975), *op. cit.*, p. 364.
33. *Ibid.*, pp. 355–6.
34. *Ibid.*, pp. 311–12.
35. O. Ozgur, (1976), *op. cit.*, p. 170.
36. To all these we should add that 1929 was also the year when the repayment of Ottoman debts was to begin, according to the terms of the Lausanne Treaty. Thus, the immense burden of these debts (the annual repayments of which accounted for between 13 and 18% of the state's budget) also hindered the industrialization process while necessitating the further expansion of the state into the economic sphere in order to assume a greater role in co-ordinating and expanding the national economy.

3. State Capitalism and National Industrialization in the 1930s

The adverse conditions brought by the world economic crisis at the end of the 1920s and early 1930s made it necessary for the Turkish state to take an even more direct role in the national economy to counteract the impact of the metropolitan depression. In future the state would play a central role in the industrialization and capital accumulation process by replacing the small, weak, and incapacitated national industrial bourgeoisie. In this chapter we will examine the policies of the Kemalist state in both industry and agriculture in the 1930s and assess their relative success in accelerating the development of capitalism in Turkey.

The Industrial Sector

The consolidation of the state's role in the national industrialization process in the early 1930s occurred after Turkey had gained control over its customs and established a protectionist customs policy designed to encourage domestic production. While immediate measures were taken to protect the Turkish economy in the early 1930s, the long-term objective of the Kemalist leadership was to establish and manage state-owned enterprises that would form the basis of the nation's industrial economy until the vulnerability of the Turkish economy had been overcome and the foundations of a strong national economy firmly laid. Following the initial restructuring of the local economy through the regulation of foreign trade (by which control over the inflow and outflow of currency was to be assured),[1] the Kemalist leadership began to formulate a national industrial development policy. This would put the state in the forefront of planning and implementing a programme to accelerate the development of capitalism in Turkey – a process which had failed in the initial post-independence period in the 1920s. Before examining the industrialization process during this period in detail, we need to examine briefly several parallel developments that complemented Turkish industrialization efforts during the 1930s: the process of nationalization of foreign firms; the First and Second Five-Year Development Plans; the establishment of new state banks and agencies to finance and carry out development projects; and external financial and technical assistance.

Nationalization of Foreign Firms

In an effort to resolve Turkey's balance of payments crisis, resulting from the deteriorating terms of trade following the metropolitan Depression of 1929, the state launched an all-out campaign of nationalization of foreign firms throughout the 1930s.[2] The first signs of a broad-based nationalization policy came with the state takeover of the main railways, utilities, transportation, and port facilities in the early 1930s.[3] This was followed by the nationalization of dozens of mines and factories owned by foreign capital in the latter half of the decade and early 1940s. Table 4 presents a partial list of foreign firms affected by the nationalization policy in the period 1931–1944, indicating the amount of compensation.

Table 4
Foreign Firms Affected by the Kemalist State's Nationalization Policy 1931–1944

Firms Bought by the State	*Date of Purchase, Law No., and Amount of Compensation*
Mudanya-Bursa Railway Co. T.A.S.*	May 30, 1931, Law No. 1815, 50,000 Turkish lira.
Istanbul Water Co. T.A.S.	May 20, 1933, Law No. 2198, with the payment of 1,300,183 French francs per year starting in 1933 until the expiry of the concession, and its transfer to the Municipality of Istanbul.
Izmir Harbour Co.	June 12, 1933, Law No. 2309. The Izmir port facilities, along with the tramway lines servicing the port, were transferred to the state for 7,827,690 French francs.
Izmir Kasaba ve Temdidi (Izmir-Afyon and Manisa-Bandirma) Railways	May 31, 1934, Law No. 2487, 162,468,000 French francs.
Istanbul Harbour, Dock and Warehouse Co. T.A.S.	December 23, 1934, Law No. 2659, with the payment of 1,400,000 French francs during the first three years and 31,580,138 French francs in the subsequent 40 years, at an annual interest rate of 7.5%.
Aydin Railway Co.	May 30, 1935, Law No. 2745, 1,825,840 British pounds.
Istanbul Telephone Co. T.A.S.	June 13, 1936, Law No. 3026,

	800,000 British pounds.
Eregli (Coal Mining) Co.	March 31,1937, Law No. 3146. The company's port facilities in Eregli, on the Black Sea Coast, its Zonguldak-Catalagzi rail transport lines, and its Zonguldak coal mine operations were transferred to the state in return for 3,500,000 Turkish lira.
Sark (Orient) Railway Co. T.A.S.	April 26, 1937, Law No. 3156, 20,760,000 Swiss francs.
Izmir Telephone Co. T.A.S.	April 25, 1938, Law No. 3375, 1,200,000 Turkish lira.
Uskudar & Kadikoy T.A.S.	April 11, 1938, Law No. 3359, 400,000 Turkish lira.
Istanbul Electric Co. T.A.S.	April 22, 1938, Law No. 3480, 1,873,000 British pounds.
Istanbul Tramway Co.	June 12, 1939, Law No. 3642, 169,000 British pounds.
Istanbul Subway Co. T.A.S.	June 12, 1939, Law No. 3643, 175,000 Turkish lira.
Ankara Electric, Ankara Natural Gas, and Adana Electric Companies T.A.S.	July 5, 1939, Law No. 3688, 6,616,131 Turkish lira.
Bursa and Muttehit Electric Companies T.A.S.	July 5, 1939, Law No. 3689, 295,110 British pounds.
Ilica Iskele-Palamutluk Railway Co. T.A.S.	September 22, 1941, Law No. 4127, 10,000 Turkish lira.
Izmir Tramway and Electric Co. T.A.S.	July 19, 1943, Law No. 4483, 10,223,800 Swiss francs.
Izmir Water Co. T.A.S.	June 5, 1944, Law No. 4583, for the equivalent (in Turkish Lira) of 1,399,157 Swiss francs.

* *Turk Anonim Sirketi,* (Turkish Joint-Stock Company), given in abbreviated form, T.A.S.

Source: M. Selik, *Turkiye'de Yabanci Ozel Sermaye,* (Foreign Private Capital in Turkey), (Ankara: Siyasal Bilgiler Fakultesi, 1961), pp. 3–10, cited in D. Avcioglu, *Turkiye'nin Duzeni,* pp. 454–6.

In addition to the nationalization of these foreign firms, the Keciborlu Sulphur Mine Concession, which was granted to French (and later Italian) capital following the War of National Liberation, was annulled in 1932. Also the 1.5 million T.L.-valued 50% share of German capital in the Ergani Copper Company, T.A.S., was bought up by the state on June 11, 1936 (Law No. 3034) with 850,000 T.L. compensation.[4] In 1939, the State Treasury took over the Kurvarshan Copper Mine Operations of the (German-owned) Siemens Corporation, due to the company's accumulated unpaid tax debts. And in 1940, the state bought up the Bomonti and Nektar beer factories for 400,000 T.L. The monopoly concession on matches, granted to the American-Turkish Investment Corporation in return for a loan of US$10 million at 6½% interest (in accordance with Law No. 1722, on January 15, 1930), was ended on May 28, 1943, through the passage of Law No. 4426, with a sizeable compensation of one million dollars – in addition to the repayment of the balance of the original loan, the greater part of which had already been repaid within a few years after its granting.[5] Also, with the growth in capital and activities of state-owned banks during this period, the number of foreign banks operating in Turkey consistently dropped, and their role in local finance became increasingly restricted to the commercial and non-industrial sectors of the national economy.[6]

The nationalization policy of the 1930s and early 1940s played an important role in strengthening the Turkish economy. It virtually ended the outflow of capital, hence improving the country's balance of payments, and, with the expansion of the state into different branches of the nation's industrial economy, it opened the way to state planning to increase production and to accelerate the process of independent capitalist industrialization. It was within this structural framework, and in the light of the significant achievements of planned development in the Soviet Union, coupled with the considerable aid and protection the USSR provided Turkey during this period (of which we shall have more to say later) that the state began to formulate, and soon thereafter implement, the First and Second Five Year Industrial Development Plans during the 1930s. It was by means of these Plans that the state began to make significant progress in national industrialization.

The First and Second Five Year Industrial Development Plans

The intensification of the state's role in the national economy and the shift in its economic policy to assume a direct role as entrepreneur in the early 1930s led the state to adopt a systematic approach to industrialization, namely the adoption of state planning similar to that already at work in Turkey's northern neighbour, the Soviet Union.[7] The formulation of a Five Year Development Plan in accordance with the economic objectives of the Kemalist leadership began to take shape in 1932 with the creation of the *Devlet Sanayi Ofisi* (State Office of Industry) and its sister organization, the *Sanayi Kredi Bankasi* (Industrial Credit Bank), which together replaced the *Sanayi ve Maadin Bankasi* (Industrial and Mineral Bank) that had been created earlier to aid and encourage Turkish private capital.

The *Devlet Sanayi Ofisi* (DSO), in co-operation with the *Sanayi Kredi Bankasi* (SKB), began soon after its creation to assume the task of formulating and co-ordinating the First Five Year Industrial Development Plan. To do this, it began to expand through government channels its diplomatic relations with the Soviet Union in the hope of securing useful technical and financial aid (and military protection against imperialist intervention) to start the national industrialization programme. In May 1932, Prime Minister Ismet Inonu, along with the Turkish Foreign Minister, made a trip to the Soviet Union to study Soviet industrialization and to sign a technical and credit agreement with the USSR, in which Turkey was granted a loan for the partial financing of the First Five Year Plan.

This loan equivalent to US$8,000,000 for twenty years was interest free.[8] It went into effect in 1934, took the form of machinery and equipment at the choice of the Turkish Government. The prices for these supplies were fixed according to world prices, and Turkey undertook to repay the loan by its own exports to the Soviet Union.[9] To administer the loan and the placing of machinery orders, the Soviet Union established the Turkstroj Agency, headed by senior officials of the Ministry of Industry.

> The Turkish industrial delegation to Russia entered into negotiations with 'Turkstroj' concerning the construction and equipment of new industrial enterprises. 'Turkstroj' did not limit its activities to obligations arising from this loan, but continued to develop trade relations with Turkey, and on April 1, 1935, brought to a successful conclusion negotiations with Sumer Bank regarding the establishment of textile mills in Nazilli. Workers selected for new textile ventures went for training to the Soviet Union, and Russian experts arrived in Turkey.[10]

After the signing of the loan agreement in Moscow, a group of Soviet experts in development planning headed by Prof. Orlof followed Inonu to Turkey in August 1932.[11] In his official statement, Orlof explained:

> Our mission is composed of experts who work in the First Five Year Industrial Programme, and at the same time engage in preparing the Second Five Year Programme . . . We deem it a great honour to be invited here to work on the Turkish industrialization programme. We hope to accomplish the task given to us in collaboration with the Turks in a short time. We will participate in the studies made to find out the best conditions for the establishment of factories.[12]

In the same year the Orlof Mission presented to the Ministry of Economy a detailed report on the construction of industrial plants in Turkey. After examining it and find it acceptable, Celal Bayar, the Minister of Economy, approved the Report (under the name 'Industrial Establishments and Operations Report') and sent it on to the Prime Ministry in 1933 for ratification.[13] After extensive discussions in the Council of Ministers starting in December 1933, the Report was finally ratified and adopted as the First Five Year Industrial Plan on April 17, 1934, and was transmitted to Sumer Bank for its implementation.[14]

The First Five Year Industrial Plan: Although the goals set by the state for the acceleration of the industrialization process during the 1930s may seem insignificant by present standards of industrial growth and development, it was, nonetheless, an important step forward in the development and expansion of the productive forces in Turkey in this period.

The main targets of the First Five Year Plan can be summarized as follows.[15]

(1) Particular emphasis was to be placed on the production of consumer goods while preparing the necessary infrastructure for the manufacture of capital goods;

(2) Industrial expansion was to take place mainly through the utilization of local raw materials;

(3) Industrial centres were to be dispersed geographically throughout the country, and in this way industry was to be extended to the rural hinterland, providing alternative employment to peasants and agricultural labourers, and locating processing plants in the vicinity of raw materials;

(4) An extensive textile industry was to be established in order to meet local demand, save foreign currency, and eventually generate exports.

Within the framework of these broader targets, twenty new factories were to be constructed during the first five years of the industrialization programme, including a steel mill in Karabuk, a paper and cellulose factory in Izmir, a cement factory in Istanbul, six chemical plants, and seven textile factories.[16] The sugar industry, one of Turkey's most important industries and one which had received extensive state aid in the 1920s, was not included in the First Five Year Plan, but it continued to grow throughout this period.

In spite of the lack of funds in the State Treasury, most of the proposed projects were completed by the end of the five-year period encompassing the First Five Year Plan.

> Within three years, ten of the enterprises proposed in the [First] Plan had been completed and had started production. By the time the preparations for the Second Plan started in 1936, except for the Karabuk iron and steel complex and three other factories, the final studies of which were already finished, all the planned factories had been completed. The cost of the planned industries was estimated to be 44 million T.L., but by the end of the period it actually came to approximately 100 million T.L.[17]

The Second Five Year Industrial Plan: The Second Five Year Plan, submitted to the Prime Ministry in 1936 and launched under the direction of the Minister of Economy, Celal Bayar, called for the construction of 100 new factories (as compared with 20 under the First Plan) and the development of nine major branches of industry: minerals; coal mining; regional electricity plants; home fuels; marine transport; foodstuffs; earthenware; chemicals; engineering.[18] Since the development and expansion of these sectors was to be based on the utilization of local raw materials, major emphasis was placed on the production of minerals and raw materials as well as on the development of fuel and power to meet the energy needs of industry. In line with this emphasis, the need for a large increase in coal production was stressed and the construction of two new electric power stations was proposed, while a decision was also made to develop an engineering industry which would process the semi-finished products of the Karabuk iron and steel plant upon its completion under the First Five Year Plan.[19]

After much discussion and debate on various aspects of the proposed Plan, the final draft of the Second Five Year Plan was accepted by the government on September 18, 1938. The targets set for the approved programme were as follows:[20]

(1) Exploitation of the mines and natural resources of the country and the surrounding coastal waters;

(2) Establishment of heavy industry based on local raw materials, and, accordingly, the development of the Zonguldak-Karabuk area on the following lines: improvements in the railway network and transportation in general, construction of a modern port for the export of steel and coal, erection of an electric power station near Zonguldak, and establishment of a cement factory in Karabuk;

(3) Industrialization of Eastern Turkey by establishing a yarn factory in Erzurum, a cement factory in Sivas, two sugar factories and a meat-packing industry, and improvement of the port at Trabzon;

(4) Establishment of an agricultural equipment factory at Ankara;

(5) Establishment of jute works in Anatolia;

(6) Construction of a power station and synthetic oil plant in Kutahya;

(7) A meat-canning factory in Bursa;

(8) A sugar refinery;

(9) An aluminium factory;

(10) Housing projects;

(11) Development of the merchant marine through the addition of 28 ships of various tonnages;

(12) Expansion of the export of agricultural produce.

Unlike the First Plan, which was primarily concerned with the production of consumer goods through the development of import-substituting industry, the Second Plan aimed mainly at the production of capital goods. 'Mining, electricity, ports, machinery and equipment constituted its focal points'.[21]

The cost of the Second Plan was estimated to be approximately 112 million T.L. – about two and a half times more than that of the First Plan estimate of 44 million T.L. – and in the light of the experience of the First Plan (whose cost, as we saw, had risen to approximately 100 million T.L. by the end of the five-year period), it was expected that the actual cost of the Second Plan would also be much higher than the original estimate.[22]

Given the limitations of its financial resources, Turkey had to secure additional foreign loans and credits in order to carry out the proposed programmes of the Second Plan. In the meantime, the metropolitan countries had already begun to recover from the Depression of the early 1930s. These two factors, coupled with the developing internal contradictions of the regime throughout this period,[23] led the state to turn increasingly to the West for the assistance it needed to carry out the Second Five Year Plan:

> In the drawing up and execution of the two Plans Turkey required the aid of foreign experts and foreign governments. However, while the Soviet Union was the main foreign source of professional instruction, financial aid, and equipment during the execution of the First Plan, particularly in the textile branch, during the period of the Second Five Year Plan, in which Russia's role was still considerable, mainly in the electrification of the country, Turkey turned increasingly to British advisers as well as to British firms[24] in the execution of several substantial projects . . .
>
> Turkey received two loans from Great Britain at this time [the late 1930s], one of £3 million and the other of £10 million, in accordance with the London Agreement on May 27, 1938, concluded with the Exports Credits Guarantee Department. These loans were contracted for an iron and steel mill at Karabuk, to be constructed by the London firm, H.A. Brassert and Co., but they were also intended to further the general credit facilities and trade relations of both countries.
>
> The German loan of D.M. 150 million, which was negotiated in 1938, and even contracted on January 16, 1939, failed to materialize owing to the outbreak of World War II.[25]

The Second World War, which broke out a year after the Plan went into effect, interrupted the implementation of a substantial portion of its projects as the emphasis had now shifted to war production.[26]

The volume of capital in the development projects of the First and Second Five Year Plans was considerable:

> During the First Plan period (1933–1937) and the initial years of the Second Plan period (1938–1939), abruptly ended by the onset of World War II, the Turkish Government provided 311 million T.L.s for public works and services (infrastructural facilities) alone. Direct industrial investments and other development activities (e.g. efforts to increase productivity in the agrarian sector) amounted to 135 million T.L.s. Altogether, the state provided a total of 450 million T.L.s between 1933 and 1939 towards the realization of the country's development goals.[27]

Turkey received several sizeable loans from external sources to assist it in its industrialization programme during the 1930s, but the bulk of the capital expenditure of 450 million T.L. was raised locally through the utilization of locally mobilized resources.[28] And this was done through newly created state financing and development agencies controlled and directed by several important state banks which were commissioned to implement the industrialization programme outlined in the First and Second Five Year Industrial Plans.

The Role of State Banks in the Industrialization Process

The industrialization drive of the 1930s was co-ordinated by several newly created state agencies, among which the activities of two new state banks – the Sumer Bank and the Eti Bank – were of decisive importance.

The Sumer Bank was established under Law No. 2262 of June 3, 1933, with an initial capital of 20 million T.L., replacing the *Sanayi ve Maadin Bankasi* (Industrial and Mineral Bank), which had played an important role in the management of state enterprises and had participated in the establishment and financing of more than a dozen private companies in the textile, sugar, and flour industries in the 1920s. The Sumer Bank began its operations on July 11, 1933, assigned with the following main responsibilities: operating state-owned factories; planning and establishing new enterprises with state approval and with capital provided by the state; participating in various industrial enterprises; and carrying on various banking transactions and credit activities.[29] Its overall objective was to reduce the country's dependence on foreign industry by the simultaneous development of heavy and intermediate local industries, as well as handicrafts.

The Sumer Bank took over from the Office of State Industries (DSO)[30] the Bakirkoy, Defterdar and Hereke Textile Mills, the Usak Sugar Refinery, the Beykoz Hide and Footware Factory, and the Tosya Decortication Mill.[31]

> The [Sumer] Bank owned dozens of factories, workshops and power plants, and participated to a considerable degree in semi-private enterprises. The wide scope of the Bank's activities enabled it to balance losses on several projects with profits on others.[32]

Over the years the Bank's capital consistently increased, from 42 million T.L. in 1934 to 100 million T.L. in 1939 and later to 150 million T.L. in 1942 and 200 million T.L. in 1946.[33] Table 5 indicates the general scope of operations of the Sumer Bank at the close of the 1930s, including the extent of the Bank's share in industrial output during this period. With the Bank accounting for a high proportion of production in the nation's main branches of industry, the plants under the Bank's control together formed the core of Turkish industry at the end of the 1930s.[34]

The Eti Bank, founded in 1935 with the development of mining as its principal function, was the second important financial institution established during the 1930s. Its specific tasks, as outlined by the Ministry of Interior, were: the extraction, purchase, and sale of minerals; the search for oil and research concerning petroleum products; the acquisition of concessions for mines and quarries; the acquisition of concessions for the production, transmission, and distribution of electric power, building electric installations, and erection of factories for the production of electrical appliances and machinery; foundation or participation in commercial organizations to deal with the above-mentioned activities; and performance of all sorts of banking transactions.[35] Established with an initial capital of 20 million T.L., the Eti Bank's assets grew quite rapidly and later rose to 150 million T.L.

Table 5
The Share of the Sumer Bank in Industrial Output, 1939

Industrial Sector	*Share of the Sumer Bank in the Volume of Output (%)*
Iron	100
Superphosphates	100
Paper and Cardboard	100
Artificial Silk	100
Shoes	90
Steel	80
Lubricating Oils	80
Coke	70
Leather	62
Wool	60
Cement	55
Cotton	35

Source: Institut National de la Statistique et des Economiques, *L'Intervention d'Etat dans l'Economie de la Turquie: Notes, Documentaries et Etudes,* No. 988 (Paris, 1948), p. 8, cited in Hershlag, *op. cit.,* p. 92.

In addition to its central role in the electrification of the country, the Eti Bank controlled almost all coal production, copper, 70% of lignite, more than half of chromium production, sulphur, and other minerals.[36]

Parallel to the rapid growth of the Eti Bank in mining and the energy field, the establishment also in 1935 of the *Maden Tetkik ve Arama Enstitusu* (Institute for Research and Discovery of Minerals), as the research arm of the Bank, was another important step. The Institute's launching of an extensive geological survey of the country's oil and mineral resources[37] made a vital contribution to the acceleration of industrialization during this period.[38]

Assisting the Sumer Bank and the Eti Bank throughout the 1930s were two previously established banks, the *Is Bankasi* (Business Bank) and the *Ziraat Bankasi* (Agricultural Bank). Both of these were established in the 1920s to encourage the development of Turkish private capital in the industrial sector and to increase the volume of agricultural production in the countryside, respectively. The *Is Bankasi* continued to grow and help finance local private capital throughout the 1930s; it also 'entered into joint ventures with the state banks, notably in the areas of railway construction, sulphur mining and sugar production, as well as helping to develop the lumber, textile, glass, coal and insurance industries'.[39] In addition, the Bank was given the responsibility of regulating the export trade. Thus, the Sumer, Eti and Is Banks together played a complementary and central role in the development of industry, mining, and commerce during the 1930s, and were assisted in their activities by other state agencies and banks, particularly by their counterpart in the agricultural sector, the *Ziraat Bankasi* or Agricultural Bank. The tasks of the Agricultural Bank centred primarily on developing the agricultural sector and raising its productivity.

The Agricultural Sector

Throughout the 1930s the state placed major stress on the rapid development of indigenous industry, giving less attention to agriculture. Consequently, the industrialization drive of this period significantly limited the development of Turkish agriculture, relative to industrial expansion. The agricultural sector, given the resistance throughout Anatolia of powerful landlords and the *esraf,* never became successfully incorporated into the Five Year Plans and remained on the periphery of the industrialization process. Nevertheless, despite its marginal role in the nationwide industrialization programme, the agricultural sector did make a substantial contribution to the national economy through increased production.[40] And this was achieved through a certain but limited degree of modernization of the productive forces throughout the countryside, which was made possible by extensive state aid.

The first clear sign of state intervention in the agricultural sector in the 1930s came with the establishment in 1932 of an organization to purchase wheat from the peasants, storing and selling it. Set up in association with the Agricultural Bank, this organization played an active role in the early 1930s, and was later transferred to the Ministry of Economy under the name of *Toprak Mahsulleri Ofisi* (TMO), or The Central Office for Soil Produce.[41] The TMO's functions were extended in 1939 'to the purchase and marketing of barley and oats, and in later years to additional produce. The Agricultural Bank put at the disposal of [TMO] the capital needed, which stood at T.L. 17 million in 1938.'[42]

The activities of the Agricultural Bank itself also increased during this period such that by 1934 'the Bank had 54 branches and 206 agencies within the country, and 36 agencies abroad. Besides strictly agricultural business, the Bank also participated in several enterprises, e.g. the flour mill at Aksaray, the Bursa baths, and the sugar factory at Eskisehir.'[43]

Moreover, the Agricultural Bank and the government launched a new policy to revitalize agricultural credit co-operatives. In spite of the fact that laws had been passed during the 1920s on the establishment of credit associations and co-operatives, little progress was made in this direction before the early 1930s when the state, together with the Agricultural Bank, began actively to pursue its new policy. For the first time since the establishment of the Republic, this brought the state into direct confrontation with the *esraf.* Its serious efforts in this period in the agrarian sector resulted in relative success – at least in terms of broadening the base of the co-operative movement and a resultant increase in agricultural productivity. Thus, by the end of 1932, 572 credit co-operatives had been put into operation under the direction and control of the Agricultural Bank.[44]

> The main purpose of the credit co-operatives was to rescue the peasant from usury. The credits so far extended by usurers and banks, while falling short of the actual demand for investment and working capital, imposed on the peasants exorbitant interest rates and unbearable servitude. The credit societies therefore had an important task to fulfil . . .
>
> The mechanism of the co-operatives was very simple. They granted their members short- and medium-term loans, and credits were . . . to be used only for purposes directly connected with agriculture and its improvement, e.g. wages, seeds, fertilization and agricultural equipment.[45]

Although the shortage of capital limited the expansion of agricultural co-operatives throughout Anatolia during the 1930s,[46] the progress made in this respect was an important contribution to the development of the agricultural sector.

The modernization of productive forces in agriculture, through a start being made in the mechanization of the countryside, and the consequent increases in agricultural productivity also contributed to the development of the agricultural sector during this period. Throughout the history of the Ottoman Empire the agrarian sector had been extremely backward. Even as late as 1927 (four years after the establishment of the Republic), there was a total of only 1,397,000 ploughs (85% of which were wooden) distributed among 1,751,240 rural families. By the early 1930s, however, the mechanization drive was well underway, and several thousand tractors were already in operation. After a brief interval during the Depression years, imports of agricultural implements and machinery began to increase substantially from 224,000 T.L. in 1933 to 389,000 T.L. in 1935.[47]

Throughout the 1930s the state expanded its activities in the rural areas by setting up model farms, encouraging peasants (through the use of new implements and machinery in state-operated agricultural schools and stations) to adopt modern and more efficient techniques of production, and providing them with the means to purchase machinery. Farm machinery was imported through the Ministry of Agriculture, and sold to peasants by way of loans and credits provided by the Agricultural Bank.

The state's role in agriculture began to expand particularly in the latter half of the decade, such that 'in 1937 a Four Year Plan was formulated for the development of agriculture, including technical improvements, aforestation, raising of agricultural exports (in co-operation with the Second Five Year Plan), and implementation of irrigation and other water schemes.'[48] Among additional steps taken by the state with respect to agriculture during this period were: the centralization of productive forces (especially means of production, such as tractors and other machinery, but not land) in the form of regional agricultural combines (*zirai kombinalar*) through the merger of entire villages into centralized productive units;[49] the establishment of village institutes, to educate peasants in modern techniques of production (and to provide general education to the village youth);[50] the development of irrigation systems throughout Anatolia and the creation of a General Directorate of State Water Works to carry out these projects;[51] the nationalization of all forests; and an attempt to implement a broad-based land reform policy.[52]

Despite the concerted efforts of the state bureaucracy to implement these projects, many of the programmes outlined here never fully materialized. This was because of the strong resistance of local landlords and *esraf* to land reform and projects connected with it, and because of the outbreak of World War II, which compelled the state to adopt a war economy.[53] Consequently, a large number of these projects remained on paper only, and though others were completed they did not substantially alter the structure of the rural economy or accelerate rapidly the modernization process in the agricultural sector.

The limited expansion that did take place in Anatolia during the 1930s, however, helped to increase agricultural production and also agricultural income. The size of the cotton area and its yield, for example, increased consistently during the period 1933–40, as Table 6 clearly shows.

Table 6
Cotton Production by Area and Yield, 1933–40

Year	*Cotton Area (in Hectares)*	*Yield (in Tons)*
1933	161,632	27,791
1936	253,283	56,410
1940	342,636	77,115

Source: Istatistik Genel Mudurlugu, *Istatistik Yilligi*, 1942–45, (Ankara: General Directorate of Statistics), p. 241.

Similar increases also occurred in tobacco, wheat, rice, clover, sugar beet, cereals, etc. The land under tobacco, for example, rose from 35,100 hectares in 1923 to 76,000 hectares in 1939, while the average yield per hectare increased from 740 kg in 1923 to 860 kg in 1939. The share of tobacco in exports also grew from 22.6% in 1923 to 30.4% in 1939.[54] This expansion in the area and total output of cotton and tobacco, as well as numerous other crops was not achieved at the expense of other crops. The total cropped area of the country rose from 4.86% of the land surface in 1927, to 10.27% in 1934, and to 12.25% in 1940.[55]

Such developments in agriculture, especially in the case of industrial crops such as cotton, played a complementary role in the execution of the Five Year Industrial Plans. As pointed out earlier, the central emphasis in development throughout the 1930s was on the industrial sector and the Five Year Plans, while agriculture was viewed as of secondary importance. Hence, despite its relative growth during this period, agriculture played only a peripheral role in industrial development in the 1930s and early 1940s. This was reflected in a lower state contribution to agricultural investment than industrial investment during the 1930s: it reached only one-third of state investment in industry.[56]

However, it must be pointed out that the state's moderate accomplishments in agriculture during this period were not achieved through the break-up of predominantly feudal relations in the countryside and the latter's transformation into capitalist agriculture (which a radical section of the Kemalist bureaucracy hoped to achieve). What agricultural progress was made was *in spite of* the continuing overwhelming power and dominance of the landlord class, which the bureaucracy had earlier attempted to destroy but had failed to do because of its reluctance to mobilize the peasant masses from below. The regime's distrust of the masses – a characteristic of petty-bourgeois bureaucratic regimes the world over – was later to result in the coming to power of a coalition of landlords and compradors in 1950, as will be seen in the next chapter.

National Industrialization and the Balance of Trade

The industrialization drive of the 1930s, coupled with increased agricultural production during the same period, had a significant impact on other parts of the national economy which fell outside the sphere of industrial production. The most important of these was external trade. In line with the state's plans for import-substituting industrialization, a series of tariff laws were passed and put into effect in the early 1930s in order to reduce the volume of imports and, with the increased export of agricultural goods, to reduce or eliminate the annual trade deficits. In the latter part of the decade significant changes began to take place in the structure of Turkish imports, compared to earlier periods. Imports of textiles decreased from 44% of total imports to 27.5%, and those of foodstuffs from 17% to only 4.3%. On the other hand, imports of capital goods and certain raw materials essential for industrial production rose from a combined 14.5% of total imports in the early 1930s to 37.2% of the total by the end of the decade[57] – a clear indication of an economy embarked upon a path of semi-independent (import-substituting) industrialization.

In conjunction with the changing structure of Turkish imports and their general reduction throughout most of the decade:

> The Ministry of National Economy made efforts to increase exports and to find markets ready to absorb Turkish products. In 1934 a special Office of Foreign Trade, the 'Turkofis', was set up by the Ministry with the task of planning imports and exports and negotiating foreign trade arrangements . . . The export policy of the Government and the exacting restrictions on imports . . . contributed to an improvement in the balance of payments and to a temporary stabilization of local currency.[58]

Throughout the decade and until the mid-1940s Turkey had a trade surplus each year (with the exception of 1938). As the data in Table 7 show, following a 101 million T.L. deficit in 1929, Turkey's foreign trade balance took a sharp turn for the better (largely in response to the Great Depression) and starting in 1930 began to register a surplus which continued throughout the decade and into the 1940s. This surplus helped increase the country's foreign exchange earnings and with it the balance of payments improved considerably.

Table 7
Turkish Foreign Trade, 1929–45 (in millions of T.L.)

Year	*Imports*	*Exports*	*Deficit (–) Surplus (+)*
1929	256.0	155.0	– 101.0
1930	147.5	151.5	+ 4.0
1931	126.7	127.3	+ 0.6
1932	86.0	101.3	+ 15.3
1933	74.6	96.2	+ 21.6
1934	86.8	92.1	+ 5.3
1935	88.8	95.9	+ 7.1
1936	92.5	117.7	+ 25.2
1937	114.3	138.0	+ 23.7
1938	149.8	144.9	– 4.9
1939	118.2	127.4	+ 9.2
1940	68.9	111.4	+ 42.5
1941	74.8	123.1	+ 48.3
1942	144.7	165.0	+ 20.3
1943	203.0	257.2	+ 54.2
1944	164.4	232.5	+ 68.1
1945	126.2	218.9	+ 92.7

Source: United Nations, Statistical Office, *Yearbook of International Trade Statistics, 1950* (New York: United Nations, 1951), Table 1, p. 149.

While the state-induced capitalist development of the 1930s significantly improved Turkey's overall economic position and placed the country on a favourable footing with respect to industrialization, it at the same time sharpened the contradictions inherent in the system, which soon gave way to a qualitatively different form of development than that experienced under the state capitalist regime. We will examine these contradictions at length in the next chapter.

References

1. The importation of various consumer items susceptible to speculation, such as sugar, tea, and coffee, for example, was placed under state monopoly. O. Ozgur, (1976), *Sanayilesme ve Turkiye*, p. 176.
2. In 1924 foreign capital controlled a total of 94 companies – 7 railway companies, 6 mines, 23 banks, 11 municipal concessions (utilities, transportation, communications, etc.), 12 industrial enterprises, 35 commercial firms. Z.Y. Hershlag, *Turkey: The Challenge of Growth*, p. 40. Capital invested in these companies amounted to £63,444,000 divided as follows:

Table 8
Foreign Capital in Turkey by National Origin, 1924

Country	%	*Country*	%
Germany	45.4	U.S.A.	1.8
France	25.9	Italy	1.2
Great Britain	16.9	Holland	0.9
Belgium	3.7	Other	4.2

Sources: Direction Generale de la Presse au Ministere de l'Interieur, *La Turquie Contemporaine*, (Ankara, 1935), pp. 208–9; B. Orhan, *Dix Annees de Regime Republicain*, (Istanbul, 1933), p. 141. Cited in Z.Y. Hershlag, *Turkey*, pp. 40–1.

3. Several important enterprises were nationalized in the late 1920s prior to the Depression, among which the Anadolu and Mersin-Tarsus-Adana Railways, and the Haydarpasa Harbour Company, (which the state purchased on January 31, 1928 for a total of 204 million Swiss francs) are notable examples. D. Avcioglu, *Turkiye'nin Duzeni*, pp. 454–6.
4. *Ibid.*, p. 456.
5. *Ibid.*
6. Although even here a large part of the import-export transactions of Turkish compradors was handled through the *Is Bankasi* (Business Bank).
7. Although the Kemalists had no illusions about the nature of the Soviet State (that it was a proletarian dictatorship), they saw no necessary short-term incompatibility between the Soviet 'model of industriali-

zation' (in its strictly *technical* sense) and that which could be pursued under the rule of the Turkish petty bourgeoisie, for its adoption allowed the realization of the state's expressed interest in strengthening the foundations of a viable, national, independent capitalist economy.

8. Max Beloff, *The Foreign Policy of Soviet Russia, 1929–1941,* Vol. II, (London: Oxford University Press, 1949), p. 41.
9. The Kemalists decided to use the Soviet loan to acquire equipment for two additional sugar refineries and for the major textile mills in Kayseri.
10. Z.Y. Hershlag, *op. cit.*, p. 64.
11. K. Boratav, *Turkiye'de Devletcilik,* p. 154.
12. Quoted in B. Kuruc, *Iktisat Politikasinin Resmi Belgeleri,* (Official Documents of the Political Economy), (Istanbul, 1970), p. 19. Also see K. Boratav, *op. cit.*, p. 154.
13. This report, under its original Turkish name *Sinai Tesisat ve Isletme Raporu,* is also referred to by some authors as 'The Orlof Report'. For a published text of the Report, see A. Inan, *Devletcilik Ilkesi ve Turkiye Cumhuriyetinin Birinci Sanayi Plani,* (The Statist Principle and the First Industrial Plan of the Turkish Republic), (Ankara, 1972).
14. S.S. Aydemir, *Ikinci Adam,* p. 404; K. Boratav, *op. cit.*, pp. 154–5. We will examine the role of Sumer Bank (the major state-owned development corporation, created to finance, implement and coordinate the Five Year Industrial Plans) later in this chapter.
15. *The Republican Party of the People: Programme,* accepted by the Fourth Congress of the Party, (Ankara, May 1935); Z.Y. Hershlag, *op. cit.*, p. 81.
16. *Ibid.* A summary statement of the First Five Year Industrial Plan and its accomplishments is provided by the Iktisat Vekaleti, Sanayi Tetkik Heyeti (Ministry of the Economy, Industrial Research Commission), *2inci 5 Yillik Sanayi Plani,* (The Second Five Year Industrial Plan), (Ankara: Basvekalet Matbaasi, 1936), pp. xvii–xviii.
17. D. Ergil, (1975), *op. cit.*, pp. 448–9. Also see O. Ozgur, (1976), *op. cit.*, p. 178.
18. Iktisat Vekaleti, Sanayi Tetkik Heyeti, *op. cit.*, p. xix.
19. Z.Y. Hershlag, *op. cit.*, p. 83.
20. *Ibid.*
21. *Ibid.* We should also note here that, to increase mining production and to reduce speculation in mining concessions, 'a law was passed in 1935 which gave the government the right to nationalize all mines which were inadequately exploited by their owners and to revoke leases on state-owned mines where those with concessions had sub-leased them to third parties.' D. Ergil, (1975), *op. cit.*, pp. 456–7.
22. *Ibid.*
23. We will discuss these contradictions at length in Chapter Four.
24. Sir Alexander Gibb served as an adviser on port development, British engineers aided the development of copper mines, and British firms were active in supplying ships and locomotives and in establishing the iron and steel plant in Karabuk. Cf. J.B. Mackie, 'Turkish Industrialization', *Journal of the Royal Central Asian Society,* (London, July 1939), pp. 451–2. (Note by the author)

25. Z.Y. Hershlag, *op. cit.*, pp. 84, 94.
26. *Ibid.* The period of 'War Economy' during World War II will be dealt with in the next chapter.
27. D. Ergil, (1975), *op. cit.*, p. 458.
28. It should be pointed out that, although Turkey received 17 million T.L. in loans from external sources during the 1930s, it repayed 36 million T.L. of old Ottoman debts in the same period, suggesting that funds for the industrialization programme in this period came in reality almost entirely from internal sources.
29. Z.Y. Hershlag, *op. cit.*, p. 91.
30. A previously established state agency set up to co-ordinate the transfer of funds and enterprises from the jurisdiction of the *Sanayi ve Maadin Bankasi* to Sumer Bank.
31. *Ibid.*
32. *Ibid.* p. 92.
33. *Ibid.*
34. In addition to its extensive involvement in the Turkish industrialization process, the Sumer Bank also provided funds for vocational schools, scholarships, training and specialization abroad, and could provide aid for schools to be established by the Ministry of Economy.
35. Ministry of Interior, Press Department, *The Development of National Banking in Turkey,* (Ankara, 1938), pp. 58–61.
36. Y.N. Rozaliev, *Turkiye Sanayi Proletaryasi,* p. 29.
37. Turkish Information Office, *Turkey Today, No. 4, Mineral Resources in Turkey,* (New York, n.d.).
38. As a result of these efforts in the mining sector, the production of a number of key minerals significantly increased during the period 1929–40 (see Table 9).

    Table 9
    Output of Main Minerals, 1929–40 (in 1,000 tons)

Minerals	*1929*	*1935*	*1940*
Coal	985	2,340	3,019
Lignite (ungraded)	8	73	229
Iron*	–	–	130
Copper-blister	0.07	–	9
Lead*	7	4	18
Chrome*	10	150	170
Sulphur	–	3	4

    * Net weight of metal contents.
    Sources: Ministry of the Interior, Press Department, *Turkey on the Way of Industrialization,* (Ankara, 1937); Turkofis, *L'Industrie Miniere de la Turquie,* (Istanbul, 1935); State Institute of Statistics, *Mining Statistics,* various issues; *Istatistik Yilligi,* various issues.
39. D. Ergil, (1975), *op. cit.*, p. 455.
40. This meant a larger revenue for the state, resulting from additional taxes that such production would generate, and also a favourable balance of trade, brought about by an increase in the export of agricultural products

while simultaneously controlling the inflow of imported goods – in line with the state's import-substituting industrialization programme.

41. The TMO was established on June 24, 1938, in accordance with Law No. 3791.
42. Z.Y. Hershlag, *op. cit.*, p. 109.
43. *Ibid.*, pp. 109–10.
44. *Ibid.*, p. 110.
45. *Ibid.*, pp. 110–11.
46. Agricultural credits, extended through the co-operatives, increased from 26 million T.L. in 1928 to 35 million T.L. in 1936.
47. D. Avcioglu, *op. cit.*, p. 484. It should be mentioned that, despite the substantial growth in imports of machinery after 1933, the volume of machinery imports was much higher in the pre-Depression period. In 1928, for example, it registered 2.3 million T.L. The substantial drop in shipment after 1929 can be explained by the contraction of the metropolitan, machine-exporting economies as a result of the Great Depression.
48. Z.Y. Hershlag, *op. cit.*, p. 111.
49. In 1937 a proposal was prepared by the radical wing of the state bureaucracy (composed of Republican People's Party nationalists) 'for a bill to reduce the number and isolation of villages by concentrating rural settlements around "centre" villages which the government would provide with all the necessary infrastructural facilities and welfare services. Once these larger, more compact, state-sponsored social units had been formed, agricultural combinates would then be created by the government equipped with modern means of agricultural production and staffed by agricultural technicians. The village units would be interrelated with these combinates, and in this way production (but not landholding) would be more or less collectivized.' D. Ergil, (1975), *op. cit.*, p. 479. This plan was put into effect in the late 1930s, with the creation of 1,000 agricultural combines, but was abandoned later due to the outbreak of World War II, when the existing combines were then turned into state farms geared to supplying food to the Army and the cities.
50. On village institutes and their role in agricultural production and the rural social structure, see D. Avcioglu, *op. cit.*, pp. 498–502.
51. In this connection, a new master plan was drawn up to divide the country into 12 irrigation zones in order to facilitate irrigation throughout rural Turkey.
52. On land reform policy in the 1930s, see O.L. Barkan, 'Ciftciyi Topraklandirma Kanunu ve Turkiye'de Tarim Reformunun Temel Meselesi', (Law for Peasants to Acquire Land and the Roots of Agrarian Reform in Turkey), *Iktisat Fakultesi Mecmuasi,* (Journal of the Faculty of Economics), Vol. VI, Nos. 1–2 (Istanbul, October 1944–January 1945); O.L. Barkan, *Ciftciyi Topraklandirma Kanunu,* (Istanbul, 1946); H. Inalcik, 'Land Problems in Turkish History', *Muslim World,* XLV (1955); Y. Kanbolat, *Turkiye Ziraatinde Bunye Degisikligi,* (Changes in the Structure of Turkish Agriculture), (Ankara: Siyasal Bilgiler Fakultesi, 1963); R. Aktan, 'Turkiye'de Toprak Reformu', (Land Reform in Turkey), *Turkiye Ekonomisinin 50 Yili Semineri,* (Seminar on 50 Years of the Turkish Economy), (Istanbul, 1973); D. Avcioglu, *op. cit.*, pp.

489–98.
53. These two key factors and their effect on the agrarian structure are examined at some length in Chapter Four.
54. R.S. Suvla, 'Protection des Tabacs Turcs', *R.F.S.E.*, 1943, p. 95.
55. Istatistik Genel Mudurlugu, *Istatstik Yilligi,* 1942–45, pp. 219–20.
56. O.C. Sarc, 'Economic Policy of the New Turkey', *The Middle East Journal,* (October 1948), pp. 438–9.
57. F. Neumark, 'Betrachtungen zur Turkischen Aussenhandelsund Wahrungspolitik', *Aussenwirtschaft,* (Bern, March 1947), p. 13, cited in Z.Y. Hershlag, *op. cit.*, p. 116.
58. *Ibid.*, p. 116.

4. The Contradictions of State Capitalism in Turkey

The accumulation of capital under the state capitalist regime in Turkey during the 1930s and early 1940s was mainly achieved through the intensified exploitation of wage labour in public as well as private industries. In this sense, the contradiction between state or private capital and wage labour constituted the primary contradiction in Turkey during this period. At the same time, several other contradictions, both internal and external, contributed to increased conflict between the state and various classes within the country. The most important of these contradictions was that between the state and the *esraf,* the landlord-clergy coalition.

In what follows the dynamics of major contradictory forces that shaped the nature and direction of the nationalist regime will be examined. An explanation of the basis of the regime's short-term, limited success will be given and of its ultimate failure and demise in the late 1940s.

Internal Contradictions

The major internal class contradictions of the state capitalist regime in Turkey during the 1930s and 1940s were the struggles between the state and the *esraf;* the state and the comprador bourgeoisie, the landlords and the peasantry; and the workers versus the state and national bourgeoisie.

The Contradiction Between the State and the Esraf

From its inception in 1923, through the 1930s and 1940s, the petty-bourgeois state under the Kemalist regime encountered prolonged resistance from the powerful *esraf.* While an alliance with this group was originally essential for a Nationalist victory against imperialism in the War of National Liberation following World War I, the *esraf* continued to hinder Turkey's development along capitalist lines, and ultimately worked to undermine the power of the bureaucratic petty bourgeoisie in order to ensure its dominance over the state. In terms of active resistance against the state capitalist regime's programme, the landlord-merchant-clergy coalition was the single most decisive force that challenged and threatened the rule of the petty-bourgeois Kemalist state bureaucracy. This challenge took many forms. But essentially it meant that the landlords exercised effective control over the production process in the countryside and, through this control, blocked capitalist development which would have undermined the prevailing feudal structures and consequently their control and dominance over the masses of the Anatolian peasantry.

The conflict between the state and the *esraf* centred around the question of land reform. All the attempts made by the Kemalist state to redistribute land to smallholders and landless peasants after Independence failed, due to effective *esraf* resistance. About the only major achievement of the state with regard to the agrarian socio-economic structure was the abolition in 1925 of the *osur* (or tithe). All other measures to improve the condition of the impoverished peasantry and to modernize the agricultural sector were taken without encroaching on the interests of local landlords – for example, the distribution between 1923 and 1938 of about 25.3 million acres of unused state-owned land.

Similarly, efforts towards agricultural mechanization and the establishment of agricultural co-operatives and village institutes were all carried out without altering the structure of the rural landholding system. Consequently, the institutions and organs which had been set up to protect the peasants against exploitation were soon taken over by local landlords, merchants, or their representatives. Development programmes initiated by the state were manipulated by the landlords to serve their own interests (as, for example, in diverting public funds granted for local development projects directly into their own private accounts).

The same applied in the case of the Agricultural Bank, which was initially set up to aid the smallholding peasantry. Top positions in local branches of the Bank were held by landlords, merchants, or their representatives, who then handled credit, loans and other financial transactions. Large amounts of public funds were transferred into their hands while more and more peasants went bankrupt and fell into the grip of usurers, finding themselves in perpetual debt bondage. It is in this sense, i.e. initiating programmes to improve the condition and productivity of the peasantry while trying to avoid direct confrontation with the powerful landlords, that the state's sustained efforts to improve Turkish agriculture resulted in failure.

The first major effort to alter the traditional land tenure system in Turkey was made in 1934 with the Settlement and Land Bill proposal. In line with the land reform legislation, sections of the 1924 Constitution were altered (e.g. sections regarding the confiscation by the state of privately owned land) in order to strengthen the state's position *vis-a-vis* the landlords. And it was also in this period that the Kemalist forces proposed measures to establish agricultural co-operatives and village institutes.

While these were important steps toward the realization of an effective land reform policy, Kemal's death in 1938 and the outbreak of World War II virtually halted these efforts. It was not until the mid-1940s that the state was again able to take up the fight against the landlords and impose a land reform policy.

The decisive move against the landlords came in 1945 when the ruling People's Party introduced a Land Reform Bill. In January of that year the government submitted the *Ciftciyi Topraklandirma ve Ciftci Ocaklari Kurma Kanunu* (Law for Peasants to Acquire Land and the Formation of Peasant Co-operatives) to Parliament. Debate on the bill lasted five months and, by the time it was finally passed and became law, it had been substantially weakened and had lost its revolutionary character.

Nevertheless, even in its final form, the bill still retained some progressive aspects, and continued to pose a threat to the big landlords. The basic aims of the law, as stated in the opening paragraph of the final draft,

> were to provide land and means for peasants with none or too little, and to ensure the full and effective use of the arable land of the country. The method was to grant land to such peasants, together with twenty-year, interest-free loans for development, and other material help. The land was to come from unused state lands and pious endowments, municipal and other publicly owned land, reclaimed land, land of unknown ownership, and land expropriated from private individuals. For the last-named category, all landed property in excess of 500 *donum* (123.5 acres) would be nationalized. Compensation would be paid on a sliding scale; the greater the area held, the lower the rate. It would be paid in installments, over twenty years, in 4 per cent treasury bonds.[1]

It was this last provision of the law (the expropriation of all landed property in excess of 500 *donum*) that posed the greatest threat to the landlords. The passage of the law, even in its severely distorted form, raised the class struggle between the state (dominated by the national and petty bourgeoisies) and the landlords (with their allies, the rural and urban commercial interests and local Islamic clergy) to its highest level since the early 1920s.[2] The confrontation between the two contending groups ended in favour of the landlords who further weakened the Land Reform Bill. Thus at the close of the 1940s, the 'nationalization limit was raised from 500 to 5,000 *donums*. The distribution began in 1947 with state lands and pious foundations, and by 1950 only a few score thousand *donums* had been distributed.'[3] In the meantime, both sides were preparing for the ultimate clash and were determined to crush the power of the other – the landlords to topple the political rule of the Kemalist bureaucracy, and the Kemalists to break the economic power and local dominance of the landlords.

The first signs of the impending confrontation came with the split within the ruling Republican People's Party (RPP) in early 1946, when the opposition forces representing landed interests within the bureaucracy left the RPP to form the Democratic Party (DP). The subsequent national elections in July 1946 resulted in a significant change in the composition of Parliament such that the number of deputies connected with the civilian-military bureaucracy dropped from 47% of the total in the VIIth Assembly (1943–

46) to 36% in the VIIIth Assembly (1946–50). Parallel with this, the group classified as landlords and merchants gained a substantial increase (over 50%) in representation – from 14% in the VIIth Assembly, to 22% in the VIIIth – while professionals gained a slight increase, from 34% to 38%, respectively.[4]

The change in the composition of Parliament, which substantially weakened the Kemalists' power base, led to a series of changes, including the replacement of the Minister of Agriculture, S.R. Hatiboglu, by Cavit Oral (a big landowner), and the launching of a major nationwide campaign to attract large sections of the population toward the DP. By identifying the state bureaucracy as the main target of mass discontent, the DP's landlord-comprador leadership, with the assured backing of imperialism, began to build up the balance of forces in their favour, later bringing them to power through the national elections in 1950.

The Contradiction Between the State and the Comprador Bourgeoisie

In the initial period of the development process, the state made a major effort to transform Turkish compradors into industrial capitalists. This effort, which extended over a period of several years following Independence, was a total failure. In view of this failure and in order to counteract the adverse effects of the worldwide economic crisis on the Turkish economy, the state began itself to take an active role in regulating commerce and industry, adopting measures that were decidedly antagonistic to the interests of the Turkish comprador bourgeoisie. It assumed increasing control over foreign trade and attempted to integrate the comprador class into the national, state capitalist economy. Throughout this period, however, a large part of international trade continued to be in private hands. Because the compradors were engaged in the process of exchange, and not of production, they were relegated to a secondary, peripheral role in the industrialization process – so much so that the state could envisage itself assuming the basic functions of trade without their assistance.[5]

In the early 1940s the Kemalist forces introduced a Capital Tax (*Varlik Vergisi*), designed to tax the exorbitant wartime profits made by the compradors and big landlords. This was to open up a new source of revenue to the State Treasury, which could be used to further the industrialization process, as well as to maintain the large wartime military machine.[6]

The compradors and landlords put up strong resistance, however, and in Parliament their protests effectively blocked the Kemalist forces in their attempts to implement the tax. Consequently, the Capital Tax never accomplished its objective, but was used instead against the minority (Greek, Armenian, and Jewish) compradors to further reduce their economic power and to ensure the dominance of the *Turkish* comprador bourgeoisie.

In addition to their opposition to the Capital Tax and their largely successful efforts to avoid paying taxes on their wartime fortunes, the compradors presented broader demands in the shape of deregulation of trade, the re-establishment of close relations with the imperialist countries in order to broaden the scope of their import-export activities, and the driving out of, or monopoly control over, the competing minority comprador groups.

The natural alliance of the compradors and large landowners challenged the rule of the predominantly Kemalist state in order to expand their own class interests and to further consolidate their power. This alliance, which had found outward expression in the establishment of the Democratic Party, subsequently took state power in 1950, marking the triumph of landlords and compradors over the national and bureaucratic/petty bourgeoisie.

While the struggle between different factions of the dominant classes continued throughout the state capitalist period and intensified in the 1940s, the super-exploitation of the working masses in the cities and the rural areas persisted under the Kemalist regime. The peasants were exploited by the landlords, while workers continued to generate high rates of surplus value which was appropriated by the state and the national industrial bourgeoisie, resulting in their enrichment at the expense of the masses who lived in extreme poverty.

The Turkish Peasantry under the Rule of the Landlords

The failure of the Kemalist bureaucrats to break the power of the landlords and to transform the pre-capitalist relations of production prevailing throughout the Turkish countryside meant that semi-feudal production relations remained intact during the state capitalist period, perpetuating the traditional socio-economic structures under which the peasantry was exploited by the big landowners.

The basis of the contradiction between the landlords and the peasants was the exceptionally uneven distribution of land. The first agricultural census conducted by the Turkish Government showed that, in 1927, 1,751,239 family farmers had average holdings of only 25 decares. In 1933–34 a report by a group of US agricultural specialists estimated that there were some 2 million farms of similar size. In 1938 a more extensive survey was conducted by the Ministry of Agriculture: 35 provinces participated in this survey and the data obtained were generalized for the country as a whole. The survey reported that, of the total 2.5 million farms, 0.25% occupied almost 14% of the cultivated land, while 99.75% (2,493,000 farms averaging 60 decares each) held 86% of the cultivated land (see Table 10). Ergil points out that the 60-decare average for the latter group is seriously misleading; if a further breakdown were available (as in the 1950 Agricultural Census), it would no doubt show that a substantial majority were far smaller.[7]

The data given in Table 10 lead us to the conclusion that during the Kemalist period, some two and half million small or impoverished peasant families were dominated by a few thousand very wealthy landowning families. The fortunes of the latter were so immense that, in addition to their own large landholdings, they claimed ownership over hundreds of villages, their ownership extending over entire valleys across the country. A great *aga* named Seyit Riza, for example, owned 230 villages, while another, named Haci Musa, owned a substantial portion of the entire Mus Valley, even collecting tribute from those travelling through 'his' valley.[8] This vast inequality in the ownership and control of land enabled the large landowners to dominate the rural socio-economic structure and, in collusion with the religious hierarchy, to impose their rule over the masses of the Anatolian peasantry.

Table 10
Distribution of Cultivated Lands, 1938

*Size of Farm (decares)**	*Total Farms Number*	*%*	*Total Cultivated Land (decares)**	*%*	*Average Size (decares)*
5,000 and above	418	0.02	6,400,000	3.70	15,000
500–5,000	5,764	0.23	17,200,000	9.95	3,000
Subtotal	*6,182*	*0.25*	*23,600,000*	*13.65*	–
Less than 500	2,493,000	99.75	149,180,000	86.34	60
Grand Total	*2,499,182*	*100.00*	*172,780,000*	*100.00*	–

* One *decare* = 1,000 square metres, or 0.2471 acre.
Source: O.L. Barkan, 'Ciftciyi Topraklandirma Kanunu ve Turkiye'de Tarim Reformunun Temel Meseleleri, *Iktisat Fakultesi Mecmuasi,* Vol. VI, No. 1–2 (Oct. 1944–Jan. 1945), p. 85.

As the main exploited class in the predominantly pre-capitalist rural economy, the peasants shouldered much of the burden of development under the state capitalist regime – largely through taxation and, in the case of the majority, through appropriation by the landlords of a large part of the surplus produced on the lords' lands. The smallholding peasantry, who also had to work for the landlords in order to maintain a bare subsistence, was thus the main source of agricultural revenue accruing to the state and to the big landlords.

In the midst of feudal wealth, the vast majority of peasants lived under conditions that caused misery and suffering. Their standard of living was extremely low, average *per capita* income for the entire rural population (*including the big landlords*) in 1935 being 32 Turkish Lira (or US$25)![9] For millions of peasants the even lower real level, if the landlords' share is excluded from the national average, meant they were condemned to perpetual hunger and poverty. The then Mayor of Erzincan, Ali Kemali Bey, stated in the mid-1930s: 'the peasant has no home of his own, nor even a small patch of land. His possessions amount to nothing more than a worn-out blanket, a broken jug, and a few pieces of firewood. His stomach is often empty, and he labours naked and hungry . . .'[10]

The findings of the 1936 *Survey of Agricultural Production* conducted by the Ministry of Economy showed that the main source of food for the broad masses of the agricultural population was the plain loaf of bread: the average consumption of bread for each 'consuming unit' was 440 kg per year; meat consumption averaged only 5 kg per year. This diet was supplemented by some fruit, vegetables and dairy products. The statistics were for the rural population as a whole, however, and it may be assumed that most if not all of the meat and supplementary food sources were consumed by the landlords and rich and middle peasants.

Exploitation of the peasant masses intensified with the coming of World War II, when they were 'made to shoulder much of the burden of the wartime difficulties [with the result that] . . . half of the Turkish peasantry sank to below-subsistence level in the course of the war, and some in fact starved'.[11]

Accustomed as they were to dependence relationships with the landlord-usurers and influenced by religious beliefs and practices, the peasants were unable to distinguish their interests from those of the *esraf's*. Their dependence kept them isolated from one another and prevented the formation of mass movements which could otherwise have helped raise their class and political consciousness. Instead, by submitting to the authority and leadership of the *esraf*, they perpetuated their subordination to, and exploitation by, the traditional ruling class throughout rural Turkey.

The Contradiction Between Workers and the State and National Bourgeoisie

Given the limited scope of industrialization in Ottoman Turkey even as late as the early 20th century, workers in manufacturing industry comprised only a tiny segment of the population, not exceeding 14,000 in 1915.[12] Even in 1927, four years after Independence, workers employed in factories with ten or more workers totalled only 60,000 for the entire country. With the development of state capitalism, however, especially after the mid-1930s, the size of the manufacturing work force grew rapidly, to reach 427,000 by the late 1940s.[13]

One of the major aims of the state throughout the 1930s and 1940s was to maintain a docile labour force in order to increase production. To achieve this, workers were forced to work long hours for little pay and under unsafe working conditions, while unions were outlawed and strikes banned.[14]

In examining the wages of workers employed in various industries during the first half of the 1930s (see Table 11), we find that in almost all cases wages either stagnated or declined during the course of the three years for which we have data.

Statistics compiled by the government for the period 1935–39 do not include wages or numbers of workers employed in different branches of industry and it is thus impossible to calculate average wage levels for that period.[15] The figures given for 1939–43, however, for employees of the Eti and Sumer Banks, which were responsible for the operation of dozens of mines, factories, and plants in many branches of industry, confirm the declining trend in wages in this period. In fact, they show a very sharp decline. The data in Table 12 show that Sumer Bank workers received far lower wages in 1943 than in 1939, while the wages of Eti Bank workers (mainly miners and power workers) were reduced by more than half in the course of a single year (1942–43), from 48.5 *kurus* per day to 23.9 *kurus* (or 19.1 US cents). Wages not only dropped sharply during this period, but workers were forced to work faster through speed-ups, and for longer hours with the introduction of the 11-hour day.[16]

Table 11
Average Annual Wages of Workers by Sector, 1932–34 (in T.L.)

Industrial Sector	*1932*	*1933*	*1934*
Construction	250.4	247.8	237.6
Agriculture	170.8	174.8	170.8
Mining	362.1	262.1	340.5
Textiles	200.0	192.3	221.2
Chemicals	222.3	259.5	223.7
Lumber	235.8	192.0	239.8
Paper Products	437.6	424.1	465.0
Mixed Industries	207.3	133.6	174.8
Others	400.8	250.0	271.9
Average	*234.3*	*207.3*	*234.7*

Source: Istatistik Umum Mudurlugu, *Sanayi Istatistikleri, 1932–1939,* Nesriyat No. 156 (Ankara: I.U.M., 1941), pp. 16–19.

Table 12
Average Wages of Workers Employed in State Industries Operated by Eti and Sumer Banks (at 1938 prices, in *kurus**), 1939–43

Year	*Eti Bank*[1]	*Sumer Bank*[2]
1939	–	12.3
1940	–	11.1
1941	–	9.6
1942	48.5	6.3
1943	23.9	3.7

* 1 *kurus* = 0.01 T.L. (or 0.8 US cents).

1. Daily wages, including basic wage, premiums, supplementary payments, paid holidays, and overtime.
2. Hourly wages, including basic wage, premiums, supplementary payments, paid holidays, overtime, indemnities, and seniority bonuses.

Source: O. Turkay, O. Uluatam, and A. Isikli, 'Fiyatlarin ve Ucretlerin Seyri Hakkinda Not', (Turk Iktisadi Gelismesi Arastirma Projesi, S.B.F.), cited in Kurthan Fisek, *Turkiye'de Kapitalizmin Gelismesi ve Isci Sinifi,* (Istanbul: Dogan Yayinevi, 1969), p. 80.

Turkish workers eventually achieved partial success when the Labour Law was passed in 1936, after repeated delays by the state. The law proved to be more a mechanism to keep labour under control, however, than one that would bring benefits to workers. It did not legalize unions, the right to strike or to assemble in public, or minimum wages, but it did establish a 56-hour week in many branches of industry.[17]

Given the extremely low level of wages and the long hours of work, the surplus value extracted by the state and the national bourgeoisie increased dramatically during this period, intensifying the exploitation of wage labour. Even the generally conservative figures provided by the state attest to this fact: 'According to our calculations', concludes an important publication of the State Institute of Statistics, 'the rate of surplus value has increased very rapidly in this period [1935–41], such that while this rate was 172% in 1932, it has risen to 318.2% in 1939'.[18]

Although wages continued to stagnate throughout much of the 1930s and actually fell during the war years, prices rose consistently, causing sharp increases in the cost of living index for successive years (see Table 13). The workers' purchasing power for even bare essentials like food was significantly reduced, and the consumption of many basic food items dropped sharply (see Table 14).

Table 13
Cost of Living Index, Ankara and Istanbul, 1938–50 (1938 = 100)

Year	*Ankara*	*Istanbul*
1938	100	100
1940	111	112
1942	221	233
1944	330	339
1946	321	343
1948	330	346
1950	340	361

Source: State Institute of Statistics, *Turkiye'de Toplumsal ve Ekonomik Gelismenin 50 Yili,* (Ankara: Devlet Istatistik Enstitusu Matbaasi, 1973), p. 367.

The data given in Table 14 are averages based on the entire population. Given the high consumption levels of the urban and rural privileged classes, for workers and peasants the drops were even sharper than indicated in the figures. In fact, according to Rozaliev (who takes as his basis the government's monthly average wage rate of 47 T.L. per worker), Turkish workers were only able to purchase the equivalent of 2,180 calories in food per day, whereas the minimum amount of energy expended by workers in industry is between 4,000 and 5,000 calories, depending on the type of work. Thus, no matter how inflated the official figures on 'the minimum standard of living', concludes Rozaliev, the Turkish worker clearly consumed only half the calorie intake that is required to maintain normal functioning.[19] Under these most desperate conditions the workers struggled to survive. There was widespread malnutrition in which many faced the daily threat of starvation, accompanied by countless diseases, often resulting in early death.

Not only was industrialization under the state capitalist regime achieved through the super-exploitation of wage labour (by means of the appropriation of surplus value from workers by the state and private capital), but a very substantial portion of the state's revenues was also provided – through taxation – by workers and peasants. Corporate, inheritance, excise, and other taxes paid by the rich dropped from 46.3 million T.L. in 1923 to 43.7 million T.L. in 1939, but taxes paid by the labouring masses (mainly income and consumption taxes) increased more than fivefold from 25.9 million T.L. in 1923 to 140.6 million T.L. in 1939.[20] Coupled with rising prices and declining wages, this burden further accelerated the impoverishment of workers, more of whom sank into destitution.

Table 14
Average Annual Per Capita Consumption of Food, 1938 and 1951

Foodstuffs	*Annual Consumption (in kilograms)*		*% Increase (+) % Decrease (–)*
	1938	*1951*	
Bread and Cereals	235.5	200	– 15.1
Potatoes	12.8	20	+ 56.2
Meat	23.0	18	– 21.8
Butter and Oil	13.6	6	– 55.9
Cheese	4.2	4	– 4.8
Milk	23.4	30	+ 28.2
Sugar	16.5	10	– 39.4
Beans, Peas, etc.	18.0	10	– 44.5
Vegetables	65.0	65	–
Fruit	48.0	75	+ 56.2
Eggs (number per person)	70	25	– 64.3

Source: *Turk Ekonomisi* (March 1949) and *Zafer Gazetesi* (September 3, 1952), Y.N. Rozaliev, *Turkiye Sanayi Proletaryasi*, (Istanbul: Yar Yayinlari, 1974), p. 168.

Despite their intense exploitation and oppression, Turkish workers remained weak and largely unorganized because of the repressive nature of the state against labour organizations and agitation. Attempts to bring together broad sections of the workers under a national confederation of trade unions and labour organizations were unsuccessful and those that did succeed somewhat were soon brought under state control and supervision. The political strength of the proletariat, under the repressive rule of the regime, was insufficient to challenge the dominance of the state and private capital in order to advance its own class interests. It was not until the 1960s, and especially during the 1970s, that labour became an organized force which could play an important role in Turkish politics.

External Contradictions

Although Turkey's state directed economic expansion took place within the framework of a semi-independent national economy, it did – as we have seen – receive some aid from external sources to assist its development during the 1930s. During the period prior to World War II, an antagonism between the state and imperialist forces could have developed over the policy of nationalization of foreign firms, and over the nature and terms of foreign economic aid. The first did not lead to serious conflict between the Turkish state and the affected firms or their governments, since in most cases full compensation was paid at the time of nationalization. Nor did external economic aid pose any significant problem to the Kemalist regime in the pre-war period, largely because such aid, important as it was at the time, made up only a small portion of the national budget allocated to industrial development, and the terms of the aid provided by the Soviet Union (the main source of external aid to Turkey at the time) were very favourable to Turkish industrialization.

Beginning in 1934, Turkey's relations with Germany substantially improved, leading to the granting of credits by German firms and increased trade between the two countries. With the increase in trade (which accounted for up to 50% of total Turkish foreign trade in the 1930s), Germany was in a favourable position to influence Turkish economic policies. And in 1938, just before the outbreak of World War II, a preliminary agreement for a German credit of 150 million D.M. was reached, although it never went into effect because of the War.[21]

Despite close relations with various countries, the Kemalist regime maintained a policy of non-alignment throughout the 1930s, a policy which protected its independence and enabled it to implement its development project. With the outbreak of World War II, however, Turkey increasingly became subject to outside pressures – pressures that would threaten its independence, put a halt to its industrialization programme and impose the adoption of a war economy.

The danger to Turkey's continued state capitalist development immediately following the War came from those external forces which had emerged victorious, in particular the United States. It was the latter's world-wide expansion in the post-war period that brought about the incorporation of Turkey into the Western orbit, as a strategic ally against communism and national liberation struggles in the Middle East. The first sign of long-term US involvement in Turkey came in 1946 with the granting of a loan, the first instalment of which was US$25 million. By 1949, US economic 'aid' to Turkey reached US$181.7 million, and by 1952 it totalled US$351.7 million.[22] The United States further strengthened its ties with Turkey by extending military 'aid' through the Truman Doctrine, signed into law in mid-1947. The initial US$100 million of military 'aid' in 1948 reached US$447 million by 1951 and US$687 million by 1952.[23] During the whole period 1948–52 total US. 'aid' to Turkey topped US$1 billion.

Overall the late 1940s marked a new stage in Turkey's post-war political economy. This period witnessed the final phase of the struggle between the Kemalists and the landlord-comprador interests who, with increased financial and political support provided by the United States, managed to capture state power. The coming to power of the Democratic Party in 1950 secured the US grasp on Turkey and consolidated Turkey's place in the world capitalist system, marking the beginning of the era of Turkish dependence and satellization under the yoke of US imperialism and its reactionary internal class allies.

References

1. B. Lewis, *The Emergence of Modern Turkey*, pp. 474–5.
2. Immediately following the passage of the law, a widespread landlord protest was initiated throughout the country, and a few months later, in August 1945, the Minister of Agriculture, Sevket Rasit Hatiboglu, was forced to resign, and was replaced by Cavit Oral, one of the biggest landowners of Cukurova (Cilicia) and a major opponent of the Land Reform Bill. See D. Avcioglu, *Turkiye'nin Duzeni,* Vol. I, p. 496.
3. B. Lewis, *op. cit.*, p. 475.
4. F. Frey, *The Turkish Political Elite,* p. 181.
5. In early 1941, Prime Minister Refik Saydam threatened the comprador bourgeoisie with nationalization of import-export trade, and said: 'I am deeply dissatisfied with the import merchants. . . I will try to explain to them that their task must not be limited solely to the maximization of their own interests, but, above all, must serve the higher (public) interest. . . . If my efforts prove to be futile, I will work to bring import-export commerce under state monopoly.' Quoted in D. Avcioglu, *op. cit.*, p. 475.
6. While up until World War II the Army had been kept relatively small and defence expenditure had been reduced to 28% of the budget, with the onset of the War it was rapidly expanded and defence expenditures rose to between 50 and 60% of the budget for the duration of the War.
7. In 1950, for example, over 60% of farm families had less than 50 decares each and together held under 20% of the arable land. See State Institute of Statistics, *1950 Census of Agriculture,* (Ankara: SIS, 1953), Table 8; *1950 Agricultural Census Results,* (Ankara: SIS, 1956), p. 122.

8. D. Avcioglu, *op. cit.*, p. 481. Suat Aksoy, in reporting the findings of a study conducted by the Ministry of Village Affairs in the mid-1960s, notes the persistence of feudal land tenure practices throughout Eastern and Southeastern Turkey, where it was still not surprising to find individual *agas* who owned literally dozens of villages and, in league with other landlords, ruled over entire provinces. 'Here in Urfa', reads a recent news story on the land question in Turkey, '51 villages are owned by one *aga* and 72 by a single family or clan. Whole villages are sometimes given as a bride's dowry . . .' (*The New York Times*, April 6, 1977). Areas where pre-capitalist relations of production are still predominant today include the provinces of Urfa, Gaziantep, Diyarbakir, Mardin, Tunceli, Siirt, Erzurum, Hatay, Agri, and Elazig. See S. Aksoy, *Turkiye'de Toprak Meselesi*, pp. 107–108.
9. State Institute of Statistics, *Turkiye'de Toplumsal ve Ekonomik Gelismenin 50 Yili*, (Ankara: Devlet Istatistik Enstitusu Matbaasi, 1973), p. 241.
10. Quoted in S. Aksoy, *op. cit.*, pp. 108–109.
11. D Ergil, (1975), *op. cit.*, pp. 485–6.
12. State Institute of Statistics, *op. cit.*, Table 19, p. 38.
13. Y.N. Rozaliev, *Turkiye Sanayi Proletaryasi*, p. 63. While workers in manufacturing industry numbered less than half a million, the size of the industrial proletariat as a whole was substantially larger, numbering 643,000. *Ibid.*, p. 57.
14. H. Kivilcimli, *Turkiye'de Isci Sinifinin Sosyal Varligi*, (Istanbul, 1935).
15. Based on Aydemir's unofficial figures on total workers in Turkey in 1935 and 1938, Fisek puts the average annual wages of workers in all industries at 196.7 and 249.3 T.L. respectively (the former indicating a further decline compared to 1934 levels, while the latter reflected a slight increase over the 1932 average). See K. Fisek, *Turkiye'de Kapitalizmin Gelismesi ve Isci Sinifi*, p. 75.
16. O. Ozgur, (1972) *Turkiye'de Kapitalizmin Gelismesi*, p. 96. As a result, industrial accidents almost tripled during this period – from 4,691 in 1937 to 11,958 in 1943. Y.N. Rozaliev, *op. cit.*, p. 118.
17. According to Article 14 of the Labour Law, 48- and 56-hour work weeks 'are taken as the base'; in line with Article 37, the work week could be further extended if employers so wished, provided they obtained permission from the Regional Directorate of Employment, M. Gorkey, *Is Kanunu Ile Ilgili Kararname*, No. 63, p. 159. Moreover, as Article 6 clarifies, in certain branches of industry the work day would be designated as 11 hours, with no days off. Thus, the document continues, 'in general, a work week could be extended to 77 hours, whenever the need arises.' *Ibid.* This was put into effect in all major state-run industries soon after the outbreak of the Second World War.
18. State Institute of Statistics, *op. cit.*, p. 155.
19. Y.N. Rozaliev, *op. cit.*, pp. 122–4.
20. O. Ozgur, (1976), *Sanayilesme ve Turkiye*, p. 179.
21. D. Ergil, (1975), *op. cit.*, pp. 523–4.
22. General Directorate of Press, *Ayin Tarihi* (May 1952), p. 103.
23. *Ibid.*

5. Turkey's Reintegration into the World Economy, 1950-60

With the coming to power of the Democratic Party (DP) in 1950, Turkey embarked on a qualitatively different path of development from what it had followed earlier under the state capitalist regime. The taking of state power by landlord-comprador interests, in alliance with imperialism, meant the transformation of the national state capitalist regime into a neo-colonial one, which now became subject to the dominance of expanding metropolitan monopolist forces in the post-war period.

In this chapter, we examine the political economy of dependent development in Turkey under the new neo-colonial regime and outline the process of Turkish reintegration into the world capitalist system in the 1950s – a process which has consolidated Turkey's dependence on the centres of Western capitalism and assured the dominance of big landlords and the comprador bourgeoisie in Turkish politics.

The Democratic Party Dismantles the State Capitalist Economy

Shortly after the Democratic Party took office in 1950, the all-time champion of comprador interests, the founder of *Is Bankasi* (the Business Bank) and the third President of Turkey, Celal Bayar, and his political partner, Prime Minister Adnan Menderes, a leading figure in the DP movement in the mid-1940s and a big landowner in Western Turkey, began a process of dismantling the national economy built under the Kemalist regime during the 1930s. Their main objective, in line with landlord-comprador interests and the recommendations of the International Bank for Reconstruction and Development (IBRD or World Bank),[1] was to transfer state enterprises to the private sector, and, in this way, to return to the 'liberal' economic policies of the 1920s. Only this time, Turkish capitalists were to build on an already developed economic base which comprised a number of diverse industries created or expanded by state capital during the 1930s. In line with this strategy, many state enterprises were offered for sale. 'Under the guise of "encouraging the national industry", their services, raw materials, power plants, and transportation facilities were offered to private entrepreneurs at less than the market price. The skilled personnel trained in state enterprises began to transfer to the private sector.'[2] Thus, during the first half of the 1950s the private sector's share of manufacturing increased from 58% in 1950 to 65% in 1954. And in some areas, such as the sugar and cement industries, state resources were used for joint ventures with private capital.[3]

Despite extensive state subsidies, however, 'Turkish entrepreneurs did not invest in heavy or technologically sophisticated industries . . . [Instead, they] remained attracted mainly to food processing, textile, and earth-products industries, areas where there were already state or private enterprises operating.'[4] At the same time, partly in response to the limited growth of local private capital in key industries, but more importantly, because of its close links with metropolitan capital in both the raw materials and urban commercial sectors *and* to meet the conditions set by the World Bank, the DP regime drew up a foreign investment law so favourable to overseas capital that it was later to throw many of the key branches of Turkish industry into the hands of transnational monopolies.[5]

Foreign Capital and Denationalization of the Economy

Promulgation of the Law for the Encouragement of Foreign Capital in 1954 opened the country to foreign capital, with virtually no restrictions on amount or type of investment, and allowed it to enter into joint ventures with Turkish companies. As the Law states:[6]

> (1)All areas of the economy open to Turkish private initiative are also open to foreign capital;
> (2)Foreign capital is not obliged to go into partnerships with native capital;
> (3)Foreign corporations operating in Turkey may (if they wish) repatriate all of their profits to their home country, add to their principal investment, or invest in another corporation of their own choosing.

The penetration of foreign capital into Turkey and its close relations with Turkish capital in a number of key industries meant the gradual integration of the newly emergent indigenous industrial bourgeoisie into the worldwide production process, becoming part of a dependent capitalist class subjected to the dictates of the metropolitan transnational bourgeoisie. While the participation of foreign capital in the Turkish economy during the 1930s had been kept to a minimum, the coming to power of the Democratic Party now brought a drastic shift in policy toward foreign investment such that within the first few years of the DP regime millions of dollars' worth of investments poured into the country.[7]

Tables 15 and 16 give information on the source and nature of foreign investment in Turkey during the 1950s and early 1960s. They clearly show the concentration of foreign capital in the petroleum (i.e. raw material) sector during this period, and the predominance of one country in these investments, the United States.[8] The amount of foreign investment in Turkey during 1951–63 stood at 1.9 billion T.L., and the United States accounted for 64.5% of the total and Britain 24%. Petroleum investments alone, during an even shorter timespan (1954–63), totalled more than 1.5 billion T.L. – four times the amount of all other investment combined – with the United States again accounting for 70% of the total and Britain 28.8%.

Table 15
Foreign Investment in Turkey, 1951–63 (in T.L.)

Country	*Amount*	*% of Total*
United States	1,217,315,108	64.5
Britain	452,508,537	24.0
Switzerland	67,561,000	3.6
West Germany	61,619,157	3.3
Holland	42,759,000	2.3
Italy	13,563,000	0.7
France	6,201,944	0.3
All other countries	25,741,000	1.3
Total	*1,887,268,746*	*100.0*

Source: State Planning Organization, *A Survey on Foreign Capital Investment in Turkey*, (Ankara: Devlet Planlama Teskilati, February 1964), p. 17; Agency for International Development (AID), *Economic and Social Indicators – Turkey*, (Ankara: AID, 1965); and my own calculations.

Table 16
Foreign Investment in the Turkish Petroleum Industry, 1954–63 (in T.L.)

Country	*Amount*	*% of Total*
United States	1,073,531,108	70.0
Britain	442,755,537	28.8
West Germany	16,862,157	1.1
France	8,944	0.1
Total	*1,533,157,746*	*100.0*

Source: State Planning Organization, *A Survey on Foreign Capital Investment in Turkey*, (Ankara: Devlet Planlama Teskilati, February 1964), p. 17.

The concentration of foreign investment in the petroleum industry was the result of the passage in 1954 of the Petroleum Law. This law, in conjunction with the Law for the Encouragement of Foreign Capital (also passed in 1954), accelerated the denationalization process by transferring the petroleum industry from state ownership to private (foreign) capital. As a result Mobile, Shell, Esso, Caltex, and a number of other major oil companies came to own large shares in the Turkish petroleum industry.[9]

Despite strong opposition from the Republican People's Party (RPP) throughout the 1950s, the DP regime continued to implement a policy of complete surrender to foreign capital, not only in the petroleum industry, but also in a number of other key industries such as rubber and tyres' fertilizer, chemicals, electrical goods, food processing and assembly. In fertilizers, for example, 51% of the shares in the *Gaubre Fabrikalari T.A.S.* were held by the Fertilizer Corporation of America; in food processing, the British-Dutch Unilever Corporation, in a joint venture with *Is Bankasi,* held 80% of all shares in Unilever-Is Turkish Ltd. Company; a West German corporation, Benteler Weke A.G., in a joint venture with the Turkish-financed Muhlis Emek Company, producing pipes and pipe fittings, owned 50% of the shares; the General Electric Company, in a joint venture with *Is Bankasi,* producing light bulbs in Istanbul, owned 51% of the shares. International Drilling Company, Michigan Chemical Corporation, Foster and Whiller Corporation, Coppers Company, Inc., Parsons, Brickerhoff Holl and Macdonald, Boldon Hamilton, Pirelli, Goodyear, Philips, Pfizer and numerous other corporations were all participants in the new externally directed industrialization process instigated by the Democratic Party regime from the beginning of the 1950s.[10]

Local Profiteers of Dependent Development

Foreign capital was not the sole beneficiary of the open-door policy pursued by the neo-colonial Bayar-Menderes regime. The 1950s was also a period of *local* capitalist expansion in commerce, industry, and agriculture. This expansion, however, took place within the framework of a dependent capitalist economy. Its beneficiaries were, firstly, the Turkish *compradors* who, in addition to their traditional role as agents of foreign capital, were beginning increasingly to turn to industry through joint ventures with transnational monopolies, and secondly, the *big landowners* who, through the imperialist-led but landlord-controlled mechanization of the agrarian sector, became part of the process of capitalist transformation in Turkish agriculture where wage labour increasingly became the dominant form of surplus appropriation in some regions of the country, particularly in Western and Southern Anatolia.[11]

The 1950s was a period of the most unprecedented expansion in business activity in recent Turkish history. Prominent Turkish capitalists like Vehbi Koc, Danis Koper, Uzeyir Avunduk, and Y. Selek built their fortunes during this period of neo-colonial dependence on imperialist capital. Free from the sort of government regulation and national obligations to which they had generally been subjected during the planned economy phase of the earlier period, the Turkish compradors now had a free hand to increase their wealth through industrial production under the direction of foreign capital which paid them well for their compliance with its broader imperial interests within the world economy. Now in the hands of comprador interests tied to foreign capital, the state was no longer an agency committed to the protection of *national* capital *against* the transnational monopolies. Thus, sections of the local capitalist class whose interests were antagonistic to those of foreign capital either went bankrupt and became incorporated into the dependent economy, or were driven to the margins of existing native industry.

Similarly, in the agrarian sector. Whereas earlier credits provided by the state were at least intended to reach the small farmers, now, with the outright control of state power by compradors and landed interests, large sums of money and credits were channelled directly to the big landowners. Thus, credits provided to landlords for equipment and operational expenditures increased from 3 million T.L. during 1945–50 to 9.7 million T.L. during 1950–56.[12] By 1960, the total amount of credits provided by the Agricultural Bank reached 2.4 billion T.L.[13] These credits were used by landlords to mechanize large landholdings through the increasing use of tractors. While there were only 2,749 tractors in the entire country in 1948, the number increased to 10,277 in 1950, to 31,415 in 1952, to 40,282 in 1955, and to 44,144 in 1957.[14] And, as Sertel points out, 90% of these imported tractors belonged to large landowners, 8% to middle farmers, and only 2% to state farms.[15] As a result, thousands of middle and small farmers were driven to bankruptcy, losing their land to big landowners and joining the ranks of the rural unemployed and underemployed or migrating to urban centres in search of work.[16] This meant that an even larger area of cultivable land came under the control of big landowners who, with the increasing use of tractors, further expanded their wealth. Indeed the area cultivated with tractors rose from 1,250,000 hectares in 1950 to 3,160,000 hectares by 1960.[17]

Contradictions of the Neo-Colonial Economy

The removal in the early 1950s of quotas previously placed on imports to protect native industry and the internal market, together with the conditions governing the provision of 'aid' (which required the purchase of goods from the donor countries), brought a substantial increase in imports throughout the decade. This increase, coupled with no comparable growth in the volume of exports during most of the decade, resulted in a trade deficit which continued throughout the period (Table 17).

The trade deficit, together with the debts incurred through the foreign financing of what were still called 'development projects', had a negative impact on Turkey's balance of payments[18] and necessitated external borrowing. In addition to bilateral agreements with the imperialist states,[19] Turkey received loans from international (in reality, Western controlled) financial institutions such as the World Bank and the International Monetary Fund (IMF). During the period 1950–57, Turkey received US$55.8 million in loans from the World Bank.[20] The extension of additional credits was contingent upon the acceptance of the so-called stabilization programme pressed by the IMF. This programme, which, among other things, required cutbacks in social services, an increase in the prices of basic commodities, higher taxes, 'restraints' on workers' demands for higher wages, and devaluation of the currency, was adopted in 1958. Immediately thereafter, the IMF provided a credit of US$25 million, while an additional US$75 million was also provided by the OEEC countries.[21] Altogether, credits extended to Turkey at the time of devaluation in 1958, totalled US$359 million, with the largest portion being provided by the United States.[22]

Table 17
Turkish Foreign Trade 1940–60 (in millions of T.L.)

Year	*Imports*	*Exports*	*Deficit (–) Surplus (+)*
1940	68.9	111.4	+ 42.5
1945	126.2	218.9	+ 92.7
1950	799.8	737.6	– 62.2
1951	1,125.8	879.4	– 246.4
1952	1,556.6	1,016.2	– 540.4
1953	1,491.0	1,109.0	– 382.0
1954	1,339.4	937.8	– 401.6
1955	1,393.4	877.4	– 516.0
1956	1,140.6	854.0	– 286.6
1957	1,112.0	966.6	– 145.4
1958	882.3	692.4	– 189.9
1959	1,316.0	990.6	– 325.4
1960	4,213.7	2,886.6	– 1,327.1

Source: United Nations, Statistical Office, *Yearbook of International Trade Statistics, 1950,* (New York: United Nations, 1951), Table 1, p. 149; *1975,* Table 4, p. 975.

Continuous foreign borrowing and expansion of credit during this period meant an ever-increasing external debt. Whereas Turkey's total foreign debt of 187 million T.L. in 1939 had reached 775 million T.L. in 1950, it soared to over 5 billion T.L. by 1960.[23] Together with internal debt, Turkey's total public debt reached nearly 10 billion T.L. in 1960.[24] The growing amount of debt also meant the allocation of sizeable funds from the State Treasury to cover mounting debt service charges. This amounted to 209 million T.L. in 1951–52, 244 million T.L. in 1955–56, and 318 million T.L. in 1959–60.[25]

Turkey's membership in the NATO and CENTO military pacts (both of which it joined when they were set up when the Cold War arose after World War II) posed an additional burden on the national budget. Although in return for its participation Turkey received US$2.4 billion in 'aid' from the United States between 1951 and 1960 (with over US$1.4 billion of it allocated for military purposes),[26] the money spent by the Turkish Government on projects connected with these operations (such as the construction of air bases, roads, ports, etc.; the purchase of military aircraft, weapons, ammunition, and spare parts from the United States and other NATO countries; and meeting the expenses of US military personnel stationed in Turkey) far surpassed this amount, causing severe difficulties in balancing its budget. During the 1950s, money allocated to military spending reached 34% of the national budget.[27] If we add to this figure expenses incurred by military training, military hospitals, and other related defence expenditures, total military spending in fact reached nearly one-half of the entire national budget during this period,[28] substantially higher than the amount spent on defence in the 1930s.

The burden of debt and debt service charges, together with mounting military expenditures, resulted in a budgetary crisis which necessitated further borrowing from the outside. Trapped in this debt cycle, the imperialist-financed dependent Turkish economy and state thus became mortgaged to the metropolitan countries and to metropolitan-controlled international banks.

The Condition of the Working Class Under the Neo-Colonial Regime

While the neo-colonial economy of the 1950s enriched the landlords, compradors and foreign capital, it brought ruin to the working class and the labouring masses in general. It also ushered in a period of externally financed industrialization that led to a substantial rise in industrial production throughout this period.[29] With the growth and expansion of industry, the number of workers employed by these industries also increased over time.

Growth of the Working Class and Unionization

There were 643,000 industrial workers in Turkey in 1951. By 1960, this number had risen to 975,509 – a 52% increase over the 10-year period.[30] The proportion of industrial workers to the total labour force grew from 5.1% in 1950 to 7.5% in 1960. And if we add to these figures workers employed in other sectors of the economy, the size of the working class as a whole becomes much greater, totalling 2,437,135 or 18.7% of the labour force in 1960.[31]

However, despite the upsurge in business activity, the capital-intensive dependent economy set up by the transnational monopolies was nevertheless unable to absorb the large migrant population of dispossessed peasant families. The mechanization of the agricultural sector, which benefited the large landowners, drove many small and middle peasants into bankruptcy, and led to massive unemployment and underemployment in the countryside. This forced many to migrate to the cities and towns in search of work. The massive nature of this migration, compared to the number of new (unskilled) employment opportunities in the major industrial centres, led to a great upsurge in unemployment in the urban areas as well. As early as 1951, it was estimated that there were over a million unemployed in the towns as a consequence of this migration.[32] This represented over 8% of the total labour force and over 50% of the labour force in urban areas.[33]

The condition of workers who were fortunate enough to find employment did not improve under the neo-colonial regime. Their wages were very low, in fact well below subsistence. And the small gains they were able to make through unionization were wiped out by spiralling inflation. The struggle of workers to improve their conditions was first manifested through widespread unionization in the various sectors of industry. Along with the growth in numbers of workers during this period, so too the number of unionized workers multiplied rapidly. As Table 18 shows, while the number of workers as a whole increased by 113% between 1948 and 1958, the increase in the number of unionized workers during the same period was 405%! Accordingly, the percentage of unionized workers in Turkey increased from 15.8% in 1948 to 37.4% in 1958.

Table 18
The Trade Union Movement in Turkey, 1948–58 (1948=100)

Year	*% of Workers Unionized*	*Increase in Number of Workers*	*Increase in Number of Unionized Workers*
1948	15.78	100	100
1950	20.86	113	150
1952	26.61	148	250
1954	30.92	177	347
1956	32.41	196	402
1958	37.45	213	505

Source: K. Fisek, *Turkiye'de Kapitalizmin Gelismesi ve Isci Sinifi,* p. 87.

Wage Levels, Inflation, and the Rate of Exploitation

As a result of forming trade unions, workers who were organized in various sectors of industry but principally manufacturing and mining were able to demand and secure more favourable wage contracts. Despite increases in money wages, however, the high rate of inflation during this period cancelled out these gains, permitting only a slight increase, and in some branches a reduction, in real wages. Thus, as Tables 19 and 20 show, the real wages of workers during the period 1955–59 remained unchanged or declined in most branches of industry. Only in a few branches was there a slight increase. The annual real gain in average daily wages in all industry (Table 19) averaged a mere 0.5% during this period.[34]

Moreover, of the various branches of manufacturing industry, tobacco workers were the lowest paid, and workers in machinery and equipment production (i.e. the capital goods sector) were among those whose real wages had declined (see Table 20).

As mentioned earlier a key factor contributing to the stagnation and decline in real wages of workers in Turkey during the 1950s was the high rate of inflation during the latter half of the decade. As Table 21 shows, the rate of inflation averaged over 15% a year during 1956–59, reaching 25% in 1959.

While the real wages of most workers stagnated or declined during this period, workers were also forced to work faster through speed-ups, and for longer hours with overtime at low pay.[35] Thus, according to Yurukoglu's calculations, the mass of surplus value in the manufacturing industry grew from 419,062,000 T.L. in 1950 to 3,365,847,000 T.L. in 1959 – or by 703%.[36] And the rate of exploitation in the manufacturing sector during this period was some 300–360%.[37] If we add to this the widespread use of child labour, women workers and other unorganized sections of the working class whose wages were lower than those of manufacturing workers, the rate of exploitation of the working class *as a whole* would in fact be much higher.[38]

Fulfilment of Basic Needs: Nutrition and Housing

To capture the full dimensions of the condition of the working class in Turkey in the 1950s, we must also find out the degree to which its basic needs were met.

With respect to nutrition, a recent publication of the Turkish Teachers Association, entitled *The Question of Nutrition in Turkey*, states that 'The minimum daily intake necessary to protect the health of an individual is 150g of meat, half a kilo of milk, one egg, 300g of fruits and vegetables, about 200g of cereal, and a sufficient amount of oil and sugar.'[39] The cost of these items at the end of the 1950s (1959, to be precise) was 3.10 T.L.[40] Taking the official figure of 5.07 as the average number of people per family in cities in Turkey as our base,[41] this means that in 1959 a five-member worker's family had to spend 15.50 T.L. a day on food alone. Yet the average daily *gross* wage for an insured industrial worker in 1959 was only 13.06 T.L., while it was as little as 10.32 T.L. for a mine worker and 9.20 T.L. for a tobacco worker (and these averages include the earnings of salaried employees as well). Setting aside the cost of shelter, clothing, and utilities, transportation expenses and the payment of taxes, the wages received by workers were not even enough to cover the cost of their family's minimum daily food requirements! This means that the wages of workers in Turkey during this period were *far below the level of subsistence.* As a result, thousands of workers were undernourished and were forced to live in insanitary, temporary slum dwellings, or *gecekondus* as they are known in Turkey, with no electricity, running water, or sewage systems.

Table 19
Average Daily Wages* by Sector 1955–59*** (1955 = 100)

	1955			*1956*			*1957*			*1958*			*1959*			*Average Annual*
	Money		*Real***	*Money*		*Real*	*Money*		*Real*	*Money*		*Real*	*Money*		*Real*	*Increase in Real*
Sector	*Wages*		*Wages*	*Wages*		*Wages*	*Wages*		*Wages*	*Wages*		*Wages*	*Wages*		*Wages*	*Wages (1956–59)*
	T.L.	*I*	*I*	*T.L.*	*I*	*I*	*T.L.*	*I*	*I*	*T.L.*	*I*	*I*	*T.L.*	*I*	*I*	
Manufacturing	6.80	100	100	7.87	116	103	8.97	132	104	10.86	160	112	13.17	194	109	+ 2.2%
Mining and Quarrying	5.43	100	100	6.62	122	108	7.65	141	111	8.57	158	111	10.32	190	107	+ 1.8%
Construction	8.17	100	100	9.19	112	99	10.04	123	97	11.41	140	98	13.99	171	96	– 1.0%
Transport, Storage, and Communications	8.62	100	100	8.61	100	88	9.85	114	90	11.43	132	93	14.76	171	96	– 0.8%
Average (all industry)	7.25	100	100	8.07	112	99	9.13	126	99	10.57	146	103	13.06	180	102	+ 0.5%

* Including salaries. All wages and wage indices, including real wage indices, are based on *gross* wages, i.e. wages before the deduction of taxes and social security contributions.

** Real wage indices were obtained by dividing money wage indices (derived from ILO data given in T.L.) by cost of living indices averaged for Ankara and Istanbul as provided in Table 21.

Source: International Labour Organization, *Year Book of Labour Statistics, 1965*, (Geneva: International Labour Office, 1965), Tables 20, 21, 22; pp. 567, 573, 578; my own computations added.

Table 20
Average Daily Wages* in Various Branches of Manufacturing Industry, 1955–59*** (1955 = 100)

Branch of Industry	1955 Money Wages T.L.	1955 I	1955 Real** Wages I	1956 Money Wages T.L.	1956 I	1956 Real Wages I	1957 Money Wages T.L.	1957 I	1957 Real Wages I	1958 Money Wages T.L.	1958 I	1958 Real Wages I	1959 Money Wages T.L.	1959 I	1959 Real Wages I	Average Annual Increase in Real Wages (1956–59)
Food	6.71	100	100	7.78	116	103	8.43	126	99	9.81	146	103	12.29	183	103	+ 0.8%
Beverages	9.54	100	100	9.64	101	89	10.62	111	87	11.52	121	85	14.21	149	84	– 4.2%
Tobacco	4.85	100	100	5.42	112	99	6.01	124	98	7.03	145	102	9.20	190	107	+ 1.7%
Textiles	6.77	100	100	7.72	114	101	9.04	133	105	11.55	171	120	12.63	186	105	+ 1.7%
Clothing	7.90	100	100	9.36	118	104	8.68	110	87	10.27	130	91	13.19	167	94	– 1.1%
Printing & Publishing	10.52	100	100	11.45	109	96	12.92	123	97	14.38	137	96	19.03	181	102	+ 0.5%
Chemicals	8.64	100	100	10.01	116	103	11.44	132	104	13.66	158	111	16.63	192	108	+ 2.0%
Basic Metals Industries	8.40	100	100	8.96	107	95	10.85	129	101	11.67	139	98	15.89	189	107	+ 1.9%
Machinery	8.74	100	100	9.84	112	99	10.20	117	92	11.94	137	96	14.65	168	95	– 1.2%
Transport Equipment	8.89	100	100	9.62	108	95	10.02	113	89	11.81	133	93	14.98	168	95	– 4.7%

* Including salaries. See note in Table 19.
** See note in Table 19.

Source: International Labour Organization, *Year Book of Labour Statistics, 1965*, Table 19, p. 555.

Table 21
Cost of Living Index, Ankara and Istanbul, 1955–59 (1955 = 100)*

Year	*Ankara*	*Istanbul*	*Average*
1955	100.0	100.0	100.0
1956	111.2	114.3	112.8
1957	124.9	128.1	127.0
1958	142.5	141.9	142.2
1959	175.3	178.8	177.1

* Figures adjusted to 1955 as the base year (from the original 1938 base) in order to make price indices comparable with the index of money wages so that real wages can be computed, as provided in Tables 19 and 20.
Source: State Institute of Statistics, *Turkiye'de Toplumsal ve Ekonomik Gelismenin 50 Yili,* p. 367; my own computations added.

The first major survey of housing was conducted by the government in the early 1960s.[42] In conjunction with this, a series of smaller surveys were conducted in the *gecekondu* districts of several major Turkish cities.[43] It was found that, although the construction of *gecekondus* had started mainly in the 1940s and some even earlier, the period of rapid expansion was, in all cases, after 1950 and continued throughout the decade. By 1963 there were 120,000 *gecekondus* with 660,000 persons living in them in Istanbul alone. This constituted 39.5% of the total number of dwellings in Istanbul and 45% of the population of the entire city.[44] In Ankara the number of *gecekondus* was 70,000 and the people living in them numbered 385,000. This constituted 64.6% of the total number of dwellings and 59.2% of the total city population.[45] 'The densest *gecekondu* areas of Ankara', reports one of the surveys, 'are located in the centre of the city. In these areas there are 3,750 *gecekondu* houses, 3,452 families and 15,493 persons per km^2. Population density of these areas is 89.3% higher than the other inhabited areas of Ankara.'[46] In Izmir, the third largest Turkish city, there were 18,025 *gecekondus* with a total population of 99,138.[47] This constituted 24.1% of the total number of dwellings and 33.4% of the total population of Izmir.[48] The situation was similar in most large cities throughout the country. In Adana the proportion of people living in *gecekondus* was 44.9%, while it was 35.1% in Erzurum, 35.7% in Samsun, 31.7% in Antakya, 37.9% in Iskenderun, and 52.9% in Erzincan.[49]

A common misconception about the shantytown populations is that they are mainly made up of the unemployed, street peddlers and other non-productive sectors of society – often referred to as the lumpenproletariat. The statistics compiled by the government, however, paint a totally different picture: the great majority of the residents of *gecekondus* are members of the working class. In 1963, 61.2% of the heads of households among the *gecekondu* population in Istanbul were skilled and unskilled workers, 18.6%

were small merchants, 10.8% were artisans, 5.05% were government employees, and 4.3% were engaged in other occupations.[50] In Ankara 66.7% of the heads of households among the *gecekondu* population were skilled and unskilled workers, 11.45% were small merchants, 10.37% were government employees, and 8.19% were engaged in other occupations.[51] Only 3.2% were unemployed.[52] Clearly, the *gecekondus* have housed (as they still do) a great majority of the working class of Turkey.

The deterioration of the working and living conditions of the proletariat, especially during the latter half of the 1950s, was a radicalizing factor that led to massive unionization and growing militancy among workers. On the basis of their increased numbers and organization in this period, the Turkish workers' struggle began to assume an increasingly *political* character, becoming in time a class-conscious political force against the neo-colonial state.

Economic Crisis, Social Unrest, and Political Repression

The deep-seated contradictions of the neo-colonial regime in Turkey began to unfold after the mid-1950s. While the externally financed dependent economy had brought enormous wealth to a handful of landlords and compradors, it had brought misery and ruin to the great mass of the people. Small and medium businesses were driven to bankruptcy, peasants lost their lands and filled the ranks of the unemployed and underemployed, and workers were exploited intensively, paid below-subsistence wages and driven to the depths of poverty. Rampant inflation, growing unemployment and the burden of ever-increasing taxes further reduced the purchasing power of the masses, especially the workers, during the latter half of the decade.

With the general stagnation of the economy and enormous military expenditure, the burden of debt, the continuous trade deficit, and the resultant balance of payments crisis, as well as the adoption of 'austerity measures' imposed by the IMF, Turkey entered a period of deep economic crisis.[53] The government's IMF-engineered 'anti-inflationary' policy, which enforced the devaluation of the currency, further worsened the balance of trade and the balance of payments. In the absence of any favourable change in the relative prices of imports and exports, the devaluation of the Lira meant that Turkey now had to pay more for its imports, receive less for its exports, and fall deeper into debt.

The economic situation continued to worsen throughout the latter part of the 1950s, and from 1958 on it began to affect large segments of the population, especially in the cities. Inflation not only had eroded the small gains made by workers over many years, but also lowered the standard of living of those on fixed salaries such as public employees and officers in the Army.[54] In addition, the unemployment situation had worsened and shortages had become widespread. Faced with an economic crisis which was rapidly turning into a social and political one, liberal journalists, sensing the unrest within the Army, the universities and among the urban population in general, began to criticize the government's policies. Progressive intellectuals and student groups also levelled criticism against the regime. But, instead of revising its policies or answering its critics, the government resorted to increasingly repressive methods, adopting fascist-type measures against the opposition forces. It ordered the closing down of newspapers critical of public policies, imprisoned journalists who had raised questions against it, expelled numerous prominent intellectuals from the universities, and imposed restrictions on rights of public assembly.[55] And, as criticism against the regime continued to mount, it became even more repressive.

With the worsening political situation, others joined in hostility to the regime; these included opposition RPP politicians in Parliament as well as civil servants in the bureaucracy. Thus, 'confronted with rising opposition in Parliament, the press, and the universities, the DP leaders became more adamant in their determination to cling to power and more ruthless in their tactics. The efforts to silence their critics by gaol sentences, threats, and, in some cases, attacks merely increased the opposition.'[56] The regime's repressive methods caused unrest within the military as well; a number of junior officers had in fact begun secretly to organize an opposition movement within the Army in recent years.[57] Efforts were made by them to recruit a number of generals who would participate in a coup, as they thought that the presence of generals in their ranks would ensure broader support and legitimize armed intervention. This conspiracy did not result in a successful coup until later in 1960. In the meantime, opposition forces outside the Army had gathered momentum. In May 1959, an assassination attempt was made against the parliamentary opposition leader of the RPP, Ismet Inonu, while on a political tour of Western Anatolia. And in April 1960, efforts to prevent Inonu from making a political tour of Kayseri failed when the officers who were sent to block his journey refused to comply with the government's order to arrest him.[58] These events were accompanied by demonstrations in several cities.

By April 1960, the regime had become desperate. Mass unrest in the cities was reaching its peak and the Democrats only responded with further repression. More papers and publishing houses were closed down and measures were passed to control all politically related meetings, demonstrations and public assembly. In mid-April, the DP Government rushed through a law for the formation of a fifteen-man committee to investigate the opposition RPP in the hope of closing down the party for 'placing the nation's security into jeopardy'. Soon after the committee was set up, it passed a resolution banning all political party conferences and meetings, including the RPP, and making the formation of new organizations and the publication of party literature illegal. It was clear that time was running out for the DP, but the course chosen by the regime was destined to failure. Nationwide protests continued during April and led to the massive student demonstrations in Istanbul and Ankara on April 28–29.[59] Martial law was declared in both cities on April 29, and the Army was sent in with orders to shoot. A crowd of student demonstrators was fired on: five were killed and many wounded.[60] Despite these deaths, and the martial law provisions, the student protests continued and spread. Demonstrations in the streets became a daily occurrence in April and May. On May 21, about a thousand cadets of the Turkish Military Academy joined the student movement by also staging a protest march in Ankara.[61] And this signalled the end of the Menderes regime.

On May 27, 1960, a group of thirty-eight officers led a military coup, seizing key points in the government, taking over the radio station and other offices, and arresting the President, the Prime Minister, the entire Cabinet, and the DP members of the National Assembly.[62] The overthrow of the Bayar-Menderes regime was followed by a year-long trial of several hundred defendants from the DP. Fifteen death sentences were pronounced and 433 others received various terms of imprisonment. The death sentences against former President Bayar and eleven others were commuted to life imprisonment, but former Prime Minister Menderes and two former cabinet ministers, F. Zorlu and H. Polatkan, were hanged.[63] The Democrat Party period had thus come to an ignominious end.

References

1. In its report on the Turkish economy in the early 1950s, the IBRD (or World Bank) placed two major conditions which had to be met if Turkey expected to draw any funds from the Bank: (1) state investments in industry had to be substantially reduced, and (2) Turkey should seek to finance its development largely through external sources (i.e. through foreign loans and private foreign investments). The Bank also counselled Turkey to expand agricultural production, light metals, leather and forest products, building materials, light chemicals, ceramics and handicrafts industries, and *not* make any investments in heavy industry (iron and steel and chemicals) or the cellulose and paper industries. See International Bank for Reconstruction and Development (IBRD), *The Economy of Turkey, An Analysis and Recommendations for a Development Programme*, (Baltimore: The John Hopkins Press, 1951).
2. D. Ergil, (1975), 'Class Conflict and Turkish Transformation', *Studia Islamica*, XLI (1975), pp. 141–2.
3. *Ibid.*, p. 142. The number of joint-stock companies increased from 3 in 1950 to 56 in 1954.
4. *Ibid.*, p. 141.
5. The oil, electrical, processing, and assembly industries are notable examples.
6. The following is adapted from N. Behramoglu, *Turkiye Amerikan Iliskileri: Demokrat Parti Donemi*, (Turkish-American Relations: the Democratic Party Period), (Istanbul: Yar Yayinlari, 1973), p. 23. This law (No. 6224), made up of 14 articles in all, was prepared by a US foreign economic planning commission headed by Clarence B. Randall

and was approved by the Turkish Government, in its entirety, on January 23, 1954. For an official text of this law, see: *T.C. Resmi Gazete,* (Official Government Newspaper), No. 8615, (Ankara, January 23, 1954). For further discussion of this law and its implications for the Turkish economy, see R. Cenani, *Foreign Capital Investments in Turkey* (Istanbul, 1954), pp. 10–13.

7. Thus, while in 1951 non-petroelum foreign investments totalled a mere 217,000 T.L. for the nation as a whole, a year later this amount rapidly increased 100-fold to 21,654,000 T.L. And in 1954 the amount of non-petroleum foreign investments for that year alone totalled 45,874,000 T.L. Agency for International Development (AID), *Economic and Social Indicators – Turkey,* (Ankara, 1965).
8. US investments in Turkey began to expand rapidly in the early 1950s. By 1954, they totalled more than twice the amount invested in 1950.

Table 22
US Direct Investment in Turkey, 1950–54 (in US $)

Year	*Amount*
1950	15,800,000
1952	18,400,000
1954	33,000,000

Source: Y.N. Rozaliev, *Turkiye Sanayi Proletaryasi,* op. cit., p. 196.

According to Rozaliev, as of 1952, profits on all US investments were over US$3 million a year, or equal to 16% of total US investment. In calculating the inflow-outflow of capital for the years 1950–52 from the above figures, we find that the outflow from Turkey was over double the inflow.

Table 23
Movement of Capital Between the United States and Turkey, 1950–52 (in US $)

Year	*Inflow*	*Outflow*	*Net Outflow*	
1950–52	2,600,000	6,000,000	3,400,000	231%

Source: Y.N. Rozaliev, *Turkiye Sanayi Proletaryasi, op. cit.,* p. 196; my own calculations added.

And, as the size of US investments in Turkey increased in subsequent years (see Tables 15 and 16), so the profits made by US corporations also reached high levels.

9. D. Avcioglu, *Turkiye'nin Duzeni,* pp. 712–7; N. Behramoglu, *op. cit.,* pp. 120–1; I. Cem, *Turkiye'de Geri Kalmisligin Tarihi,* pp. 463–8.
10. Y.N. Rozaliev, *Turkiye Sanayi Proletaryasi,* pp. 45–51.

11. There is no reliable data on the extent of capitalist relations in Turkish agriculture during this period. Nevertheless, if Moiseyef's estimates are correct, in nearly two-fifths of the large farms (i.e. on 3–3.5 million hectares of land, out of 8.5 million hectares) production was carried out on a capitalist basis. Given that there were 17 million hectares of cultivated land in Turkey as a whole in 1957, this means that 18–20% of all cultivated land was operated by large capitalist farmers. And if we add to this figure the area cultivated by rich peasants utilizing wage labour, we would see a further increase in the percentage of cultivated land operated on a capitalist basis. See Y. Sertel, *Turkiye'de Ilerici Akimlar,* (Progressive Movements in Turkey), (Istanbul: Ant Yayinlari, 1969), p. 80.
12. *Ibid.*, p. 78. In addition, the state instituted an agricultural pricing policy that immensely benefited the landlords: the price it paid them was twice as high as the world price. The sum paid to the landowners increased from 23 million T.L. in 1949–50 to over 519 million T.L. during the latter half of 1954. See 'Progress in Turkey's Villages', *The Economist* (March 20, 1954), p. 875. This sum increased even further in subsequent years. What is more, agricultural incomes were by law tax-exempt. See O. Okyar, 'Agricultural Price Policy: The Turkish Experience', in Economic and Social Studies Conference Board, *Agricultural Aspects of Economic Development,* (Istanbul, 1965), pp. 281–320.
13. Y. Sertel, *Turkiye'de Ilerici Akimlar,* p. 77. Most of these credits were made available by the United States and other imperialist countries for the purchase of farm machinery and supplies from these countries.
14. Z.Y. Hershlag, *Turkey,* p. 356.
15. Y. Sertel, *op. cit.*, p. 78. According to H. Reed's report in the early 1950s, 'These tractors cost between ten and twenty thousand Turkish liras, roughly US$3,500–$7,000, which is a fabulous sum to the average peasant whose normal cash income before the recent boom seldom exceeded US$250 annually. This means that the wealthy peasants, or a relatively small number of absentee landlords, have bought most of the tractors and the farm equipment which they, themselves, use to good advantage . . . ' See H. Reed, 'A New Force at Work in Democratic Turkey', *Middle East Journal,* Vol. 7, No. 1 (1953), p. 38.
16. According to a survey conducted by the Ankara University Faculty of Political Science in 1954, the number of share-croppers who became unemployed as a result of the use of tractors in the 448 villages surveyed were distributed according to region as follows: Central Anatolia 1,152; Aegean 3,271; Southeastern Anatolia 1,977; Mediterranean 9,268; Marmara 1,396; Black Sea 199. These figures represent findings based on roughly only 1% of all villages, for there are over 40,000 villages in Turkey. Ankara Universitesi Siyasal Bilgiler Fakultesi, *Turkiye'de Zirai Makinalasma,* (Agricultural Mechanization in Turkey), No. 39, (Ankara: S.B.F., 1954), p. 129, cited in Y. Sertel, *op. cit.*, p. 79.
17. Y. Sertel, *op. cit.*, p. 79. The total land area of Turkey is 78 million hectares.
18. While this deficit was 33.9 million T.L. in 1951–52, it rose to 226.6 million T.L. in 1952–53, to 452.3 million T.L. in 1954–55, and to

837.3 million T.L. in 1956–57 (*U.N. Statistical Yearbook*, various issues).

19. As, for example, the credit provided by the US Export–Import Bank, which in 1952 stood at 100 million T.L. (or US$34 million). Y.N. Rozaliev, *op. cit.*, p. 195.
20. IMF, *International Financial Statistics,* August 1958 and April 1965.
21. A.O. Krueger, *Turkey,* (New York: National Bureau of Economic Research, 1974), p. 77. By the end of 1958, Turkey's quota in the IMF was US$86 million, and its paid-up gold subscription stood at US$21.5 million (equivalent to 35% of the quota). Z.Y. Hershlag, *op. cit.*, p. 147.
22. A.O. Krueger, *op. cit.*, p. 77.
23. Z.Y. Hershlag, *op. cit.*, p. 338.
24. *Ibid.*
25. *Ibid.*, p. 336.
26. Y. Sertel, *op. cit.*, p. 100.
27. While in 1951–52 defence spending was 414.3 million T.L. or 29% of the national budget, it increased to 711 million T.L. in 1954–55 and to 1.2 billion T.L. in 1956–57, 30 and 34% of the budget, respectively. In all, Turkey spent 7.2 billion T.L. on the military during 1951–60. Z.Y. Hershlag, *op. cit.*, pp. 336–7.
28. Y. Sertel, *op. cit.*, p. 100.
29. As the following table shows, industrial production rose by 77% between 1950 and 1960, or at an annual rate of 7.7%.

Table 24
Index of Industrial Production, 1950–60 (1948 = 100)

Year	*All Industry*
1950	109.5
1953	141.5
1955	154.2
1957	176.2
1960	193.8

Source: T. Tayanc, *Sanayilesme Surecinde 50 Yil,* p. 154, cited in O. Ozgur, *Sanayilesme ve Turkiye,* p. 192.

30. International Labour Organization, *Yearbook of Labour Statistics, 1965,* (Geneva: ILO, 1966), Table 2A, pp. 124–5.
31. *Ibid.*
32. F. Ahmad, *The Turkish Experiment in Democracy, 1950–75,* (Boulder: Westview Press, 1977), p. 136.
33. Accordingly, the urban population increased from 25% of the total population in 1950 to 28.8% in 1955 and 31.9% in 1960. See Ministry of Reconstruction and Resettlement, General Directorate of Housing, *Urbanization, Squatter Houses and Housing Policy,* (Ankara: Dogus Ltd. Sirketi Matbaasi, 1966), p. 35.
34. It must be pointed out that the data given in Tables 19 and 20 are for insured workers only, and include salaried employees as well. If data

were available on the remaining two-thirds of workers who were uninsured and unorganized, the average wages of workers in various branches of industry would in fact be much lower than those indicated in the tables.

35. This is reflected in the threefold increase in the number of industrial accidents during this period – from 19,775 in 1950 to 31,505 in 1955 and 63,014 in 1960. R. Yurukoglu, *Turkey – Weak Link of Imperialism,* (London: Iscinin Sesi Publications, 1979), p. 75.
36. *Ibid.*, p. 154.
37. *Ibid.*, pp. 56–7.
38. *Ibid.*, pp. 57–8.
39. Turkish Teachers Association, *Turkiye'de Beslenme Sorunu,* (The Question of Nutrition in Turkey), (Ankara: TOB-DER Yayinlari, 1975), pp. 3–4, cited in R. Yurukoglu. *op. cit.*, p. 76.
40. We have arrived at this figure for 1959 by computing the cost of each item on the basis of retail food prices in Istanbul in 1963 (the earliest year for which we were able to find data) and deducting from the total the inflation rate for food in Istanbul for the period 1959–63, which totalled 30%. Prices of the required food items were as follows in 1963:
150 grams at 788 kurus per kilo = 118 kurus on meat
500 grams at 160 kurus per kilo = 80 kurus on milk
1 egg at 31 kurus each = 31 kurus on eggs
300 grams at 150 kurus per kilo = 45 kurus on fruits and vegetables
1 loaf at 97 kurus each = 97 kurus on bread
50 grams at 886 kurus per kilo = 44 kurus on oil
100 grams at 275 kurus per kilo = 28 kurus on sugar
Total = 443 kurus (or 4.43 T.L.)
If we deduct from this figure the 30% inflation in overall food prices during 1959–63, we end up with a total of 310 kurus (or 3.10 T.L.) for 1959. For the retail food prices in 1963, see State Institute of Statistics, *Statistical Yearbook of Turkey, 1971,* (Ankara: State Institute of Statistics, 1973), Table 401, p. 427. For the rate of inflation for food during 1959–63, see International Labour Organization, *Yearbook of Labour Statistics, 1969,* (Geneva: International Labour Office, 1969), Table 25B, p. 669.
41. According to the figures provided by the Ministry of Reconstruction and Resettlement, in 1960 the average number of people per family in Turkey as a whole was 5.68; in the cities it was 5.07; and in the villages it was 6.02. According to the results of a survey conducted in 20 of the larger cities of Turkey, the average number of people per family in these cities was 4.74 in 1960. See Ministry of Reconstruction and Resettlement, General Directorate of Housing, *Urbanization, Squatter Houses and Housing Policy, op. cit.*, p. 8, and State Institute of Statistics, *1960 Housing Conditions Survey in 20 Cities,* (Ankara: State Institute of Statistics, 1962).
42. *Ibid.*
43. See the following publications by the Ministry of Reconstruction and Resettlement, General Directorate of Housing, *Gecekondus in Ankara; Gecekondus in Ankara-Gulveren; Les Bidonvilles d'Istanbul; Izmir Gecekondulari,* (Ankara: Dogus Ltd. Sti Matbaasi, 1966).

44. Ministere de la Reconstruction et du Retablissement, Direction Generale de Logement, *Les Bidonvilles d'Istanbul,* (Ankara: Dogus Ltd. Sti. Matbaasi, 1966), p. 3.
45. Ministry of Reconstruction and Resettlement, General Directorate of Housing, *Gecekondus in Ankara, op. cit.,* p. 3.
46. *Ibid.*
47. Imar ve Iskan Bakanligi, Mesken Genel Mudurlugu, *Izmir Gecekondulari* (Ankara: Dogus Ltd. Sti. Matbaasi, 1966), p. 3.
48. *Ibid.*
49. Ministry of Reconstruction and Resettlement, General Directorate of Housing, *Urbanization, Squatter Houses and Housing Policy*, pp. 15–6. The government surveys reveal that in *gecekondu* districts the average number of rooms per family was 1.67 and the average number of persons per room was 3. Nearly one-half of these units had earth floors and more than three-quarters of them had inside and outside walls that were plastered with mud. Only 10.1% of the *gecekondus* in Ankara had electricity, water and sewage systems. There was no running water in 85% of the housing units and 50% of them had neither electricity nor sewage systems. And in Istanbul, 95.5% of the *gecekondus* did not have sewage systems. Ministry of Reconstruction and Resettlement, General Directorate of Housing, *Gecekondus in Ankara-Gulveren, op. cit.,* p. 3; *Les Bidonvilles d'Istanbul,* p.10.
50. *Les Bidonvilles d'Istanbul,* p. 9.
51. *Gecekondus in Ankara-Gulveren,* p. 2.
52. *Ibid.*
53. Y. Sertel, *op. cit.,* pp. 76–114.
54. I. Cem, *op. cit.,* p. 410.
55. F. Ahmad, *op. cit.,* pp. 52–61.
56. E.J. Cohn, *Turkish Economic, Social, and Political Change,* (New York: Praeger Publishers, 1970), p. 24.
57. F. Ahmad, *op. cit.,* pp. 155–8.
58. Y. Sertel, *op. cit.,* p. 115.
59. F. Ahmad, *op. cit.,* p. 159.
60. R.F. Nyrop, et. al., *Area Handbook for the Republic of Turkey,* 2nd edn., (Washington, D.C.: US Government Printing Office, 1973), p. 47.
61. *Ibid.;* J.M. Landau, *Radical Politics in Modern Turkey,* (Leiden: E.J. Brill, 1974), p. 7.
62. *Ibid.,* p. 8.
63. R.F. Nyrop, et al., *op. cit.,* p. 49.

6. Neo-colonialism and Class Struggle, 1960-71

The economic and socio-political crises of the late 1950s, brought about by the neo-colonial policies of the DP regime, had given rise, as we have already noted, to unrest within the armed forces for several years. The hopelessness of the economic situation, increasing social discontent and mass protests, continued repression by the state, and the realization by a section of the officer corps in the Army that the Bayar-Menderes regime's policies could spark off a social explosion, prompted the junior officers to seize state power through a military coup in early 1960.

The 1960 Coup

The coup against Menderes in May 1960 had been in the making since the mid-1950s. The developing crises in the second half of the decade had brought together several factions within the Army in their general criticisms of the regime. These factions consisted of pro-RPP Kemalist officers who were discontented with the regime's 'anti-statist' policies and wished to reinstitute the Kemalist state; ultra-nationalist junior officers who opposed both the existing neo-colonial structure and the 'bureaucratic statism' of the Kemalists and who wished to establish a religious-culturalist military fascist state; and lastly a group of generals and senior officers who, while they were critical of the DP regime, wanted to preserve the basic neo-colonial class and political structure by means of minor reforms and concessions.[1] Of these three groups within the Army who collaborated to carry out the coup, it was the second – the ultra-nationalist, fascist group – that made up the nucleus of the conspirators and worked out the precise details of the intervention.[2] The leader of this group, who later organized and led the fascist party, *Milli Hareket Partisi* (Nationalist Action Party), was Colonel Alparslan Turkes. Several generals were recruited by Turkes and the junior officers who led the coup, and these were placed in key positions within the junta in order to give legitimacy to the intervention and secure a following among rank-and-file officers.[3] General Cemal Gursel, a trusted general who had fought at Gallipoli under Kemal Ataturk, was placed at the head of the 38-man junta.

Following the seizure of power in May 1960, the junta formed itself into a National Unity Committee (NUC), consisting of five generals, seven colonels, five lieutenant-colonels, thirteen majors, and eight captains.[4] Fourteen of the junior officers in the NUC were followers of Turkes. Although during the coup the military units were commanded by majors and colonels, the placement of the generals in key positions of leadership within the NUC undermined the plans of the Turkes group, as the latter soon lost control over the generals, and therefore the direction of military rule. In retrospect, it appears that the American-nurtured, pro-NATO generals were not so naive as to be manipulated by the officer cadre, and that their collaboration with the ultra-reactionary pro-Turkes junior officers was a tactical move to prevent an anti-imperialist (anti-US) *fascist* takeover and to maintain the old neo-colonial structure.[5] Given the pro-Western, neo-colonialist orientation of the generals and their aim to restore order within a multi-party framework, military intervention to them meant the realization of five basic objectives: (1) to put an end to the crisis-stricken Democratic Party regime; (2) to outlaw the DP and punish key figures in the DP administration, to dampen public anger against the system and show that 'justice would prevail'; (3) to purge the fascist group within the NUC and co-opt the Kemalist forces in it; (4) to make minor concessions to labour, to the landless and unemployed, to the press, to students and the intelligentsia, and to others adversely affected by the policies of the DP regime; and (5) to hand over state power to the victorious party following new general elections.

The first aim had already been accomplished through the staging of the coup in May 1960. The second was carried out swiftly: the DP was made illegal and all those in the Menderes administration, as well as numerous DP officials outside the government, were promptly arrested, and, within a few months of their confinement, the trial of some several hundred defendants from the DP had begun.[6] Meanwhile, less than six months after the coup, the fourteen fascist officers, including Turkes, were purged from the NUC, assigned as counsellors to Turkish embassies abroad, and sent out of the country.[7] Next, a number of concessions were made to the Kemalist officers in the NUC. Of these, the most notable were the establishment of a State Planning Organization (SPO) and, in conjunction with it, the promulgation of the First (Post-war) Five Year Development Plan. However, as we shall see later, the SPO and the Five Year Plans did not signify a return to the economic policies of the state capitalist period, but were themselves to become instruments of neo-colonial accumulation. Finally, in January 1961, a new Constituent Assembly, consisting of the 24-member NUC plus 271 nominated and elected members, was formed. A group of professors from Istanbul University was asked to draft a new Constitution. Upon its completion, and following considerable debate in the Assembly, it was ratified in May 1961 and submitted to a national referendum in early July. To accommodate the various demands of the masses, the new Constitution contained a number of progressive measures, including the right to collective bargaining and the right to strike, the right to form new political parties, press freedoms, university autonomy and freedom of speech and assembly.[8] All these rights and freedoms, of course, were defined within the framework of bourgeois democracy; in practice, they strengthened the capacity of right-wing fascist groups and parties to organize and disseminate their views while, at the same time, successive governments never gailed to restrict or ban the activities or left-wing parties and organizations.[9] Despite its flaws, however, the new Constitution seemed sufficiently attractive on paper to win approval by a vote of 6.3 million to 3.9 million. Elections were scheduled for October 1961 and the resumption of multi-party activity was again authorized.

Party Politics and Coalition Governments

With the restoration of political parties in early 1961, new parties began to emerge and took part in the election campaign. In all, fourteen right-wing and centre parties contested the general election in October. Of these, four were the most important: the old Republican People's Party (RPP), led by Inonu; two new parties, the Justice Party (JP – *Adalet Partisi*) and the New Turkey Party (NTP – *Yeni Turkiye Partisi*), both of which, particularly the JP, drew their support from the members and followers of the old Democratic Party; and the Republican Peasants Nation Party (RPNP – *Cumhuriyetci Koylu Millet Partisi*), a reactionary organization led by ultra-nationalist elements.

The results of the election were inconclusive: the RPP received 36.7% of the votes and 173 seats; the JP and the NTP received 34.8% and 13.7% of the votes and 158 and 65 seats, respectively; and the RPNP received 14% of the votes and won 54 seats.[10] A coalition government was formed under Inonu with General Cemal Gursel, the leader of the 1960 coup and the head of the NUC, as president.

Starting with the 1961 elections and until the second military intervention in 1971, Turkey went through a series of political crises, which included the formation and dissolution of several coalition governments, internal party factionalism and two attempted – but unsuccessful – military coups.

In early November, President Gursel and the military High Command in the NUC gave Inonu the task of forming his first coalition. Although initially none of the parties wanted to share power with the RPP, the considerable pressure put on the Justice Party by the generals persuaded the latter to form a coalition government with Inonu. 'The new government was announced on 20 November and the portfolios were divided evenly between the two parties, each receiving eleven ministries.'[11] The participation of the Justice Party (in effect, the old DP) in this coalition blocked the implementation of the reforms promised by the new Constitution, as these were directed against the landed interests and comprador elements which had enriched themselves under the Democratic Party regime. Confrontation between the RPP and the neo-Democrats intensified as unrest began to surface among the popular forces and within the Army. In urban industrial areas workers began to agitate for implementation of the right to collective bargaining and the right to strike, permitted under the new Constitution. Workers' protests continued and reached a high point only a month after the new civilian government had been formed when, on December 31, thousands of workers staged a mass rally in Istanbul to press the government to heed their demands. Dissatisfaction with the regime grew among wide sections of the population as its ability to deal with the nation's pressing social and economic problems was called into question. The intelligentsia and technocratic elements also became disillusioned when the concessions, gained from the generals following the 1960 coup and which were written into the new Constitution, did not yield any concrete results and remained only on paper. The general economic and socio-political situation reached crisis proportions by early 1962, and this led to the abortive coup of February 22 by Colonel Talat Aydemir, Commandant of the War College and a sympathizer of Turkes and the fourteen pro-Turkes junior officers who had earlier been purged from the NUC and exiled abroad.

The deterioration of the general economic situation and the failure to obtain concessions from the JP on the main issues confronting the government soon led to Inonu's resignation, and so the dissolution of the First Coalition, in May 1962.

In June, President Gursel asked Inonu to form a new coalition. After considerable difficulty, and with military pressure again being brought to bear on the various parties still active in politics, the Second Coalition was formed by the end of the month. It consisted of the RPP, the RPNP, the NTP, and Independents. This coalition marked a further swing to the right, which meant the adoption of a more active policy of repression against the labour movement and the left, as well as the granting of further concessions to the reactionary forces. While these moves undermined the chances of a successful implementation of the reforms called for in the 1961 Constitution (e.g. state planning, tax reform, and land redistribution), they also caused dissension within the RPP, leading to the call for Inonu's resignation both as Prime Minister and as Party Chairman. But Inonu stayed on despite the criticisms. Shortly afterwards, 'the principal technical advisers at the State Planning Organization (SPO) resigned collectively because the government had diluted the plan so as to make it ineffective'.[12] In early October 1962 there were anti-Inonu demonstrations in Ankara and demands for his resignation. This was followed by the resignation of prominent RPP members.[13]

Notwithstanding the protests of reformist elements within and outside the party, the RPP followed a conciliatory line towards its right-wing coalition partners and hardened its position against the progressive forces.

With the party's steady move away from its Kemalist principles, a section of the radical nationalist intelligentsia connected with the left-wing of the RPP began to move toward an independent base of ideological expression and political action founded on these principles. These forces converged around the weekly publication, *Yon,* established in December 1961. Throughout this period, the intellectuals and others associated with the *Yon* group viewed themselves as 'the true representatives of the Kemalist cause' – anti-imperialism, nationalism, and state-directed social and economic development. They formed an independent opposition against the conservative forces, including the RPP.

On the labour front, the new Constitution had permitted the formation of a legally constituted socialist party; and in February 1961 a number of trade unionists founded the Workers Party of Turkey (WPT – *Turkiye Isci Partisi*). Within a year, under the leadership of Mehmet Ali Aybar, the party began to attract numerous intellectuals and students, while at the same time maintaining its rank-and-file working-class base. In the absence of the legalization of the Communist Party of Turkey by the authorities, the WPT and the *Yon* group were the only legally organized left-wing forces in the country. Despite its reformist politics and petty-bourgeois distortions – the result of its open door policy towards the liberal intelligentsia and ex-RPP members – the WPT was instrumental in advancing the interests of the working class and promoting democratic rights and freedoms. As the strength of the party grew, so did official repression against it. Nevertheless, with the growing struggles of workers in the factories, mines and industry in general on the one hand and the political gains through advances in party organization and agitation on the other, coupled with disillusion among the intelligentsia and technocratic elite in the midst of the continuing crisis within the RPP and the RPP-led coalition government during 1962–63, Turkey entered a period of wider political crisis, the long-term consequences of which only became clear later. Although the labour movement and the forces on the Left in general were not yet strong enough to pose any immediate threat to the bourgeois regime, they were nonetheless steadily gaining momentum, and the regime had no intention of taking any chances. 'In this atmosphere the Assembly set up an all-party Commission to Combat Communism (*Komunizmle Mucadele Komisyonu*) on 11 January 1963. This was followed later in the year by the countrywide reactionary organization known as the Association to Combat Communism (*Komunizmle Mucadele Dernegi*).'[14]

In the meantime, the fourteen exiled pro-Turkes fascist officers were granted permission to return to Turkey and in early 1963 they began to arrive. The arrival of Turkes himself in late February gave an added incentive to the pro-Turkes officers in the Army to try and stage another coup. Colonel Aydemir attempted his second *putsch* in May, but, as in his previous try a year earlier, the attempt failed. This time, there were extensive arrests and in July 1964 Aydemir and three others were executed. Turkes, too, was arrested, on suspicion of possible connections with Aydemir's abortive coup, but the charges were later dropped and he was released. The events of May 1963 and the general unrest among wide sections of the population led to the imposition of martial law in Ankara, Istanbul, and Izmir. It remained in effect until the middle of the following year. Assisted by the martial law commanders and the military High Command in 'maintaining law and order', the Second Coalition survived until the local elections in November. The results of the local and municipal elections of November 17, 1963, were disappointing to the RPP's coalition partners, the NTP and the RPNP, while the Justice Party did better than expected. The RPP itself polled 37.5% of the votes, and the JP polled 46.2%, the NTP 6.5%, and the RPNP 2.6%.[15] Following their electoral setback, the two minor parties decided to withdraw from the coalition. This led to the resignation of Inonu as Prime Minister in early December, and the Second Coalition came to an abrupt end.

Ragip Gumuspala, chairman of the Justice Party, was asked to form a new government. But when he failed to form a cabinet, the task was given to Inonu once again. The NTP and RPNP declined to enter a new coalition with the RPP, and Inonu went ahead and formed a cabinet with the support of Independents.

Despite its weakness, the Third Coalition remained intact throughout 1964, as the Cyprus crisis, which threatened to precipitate open war between Turkey and Greece, came to the aid of the government and helped secure national support for its policies. In the meantime, Suleyman Demirel, a representative of the Morrison Corporation, an American firm, was elected the new leader of the Justice Party in November 1964. Using the budget debate as a springboard to capture political power, Demirel succeeded in obtaining the necessary majority to block approval of the budget. Inonu then submitted his resignation, and the coalition government collapsed once again.

Suat Hayri Urguplu, an Independent Senator from Kayseri, who had run on the JP list in 1961, was asked to form a caretaker government until the general elections in October 1965. The government formed by Urguplu in February was a coalition made up of four right-wing parties with the Justice Party as the *de facto* dominant partner. It included the JP, the NTP, the RPNP, the NP, as well as the Independents. Repression against the Left and the progressive forces intensified under this Fourth Coalition government as the reactionary grouping of rightist forces led by the JP began to whip up a 'red scare' throughout the country. In its hysterical campaign to secure victory in the forthcoming general elections, the JP and its comprador leader Demirel even went so far as to accuse the centrist RPP of 'Leftism' on account of their alleged 'goal . . . to bring about a complete change in the established social order, . . . [as] they assailed private ownership, wealth, profits, reputations; in short everything'![16]

With such demagogy and assisted by large sums of money poured into its election campaign by the US and other imperialist interests,[17] the JP secured a decisive victory in the general elections in October 1965. It polled 52.9% of the vote and won 240 seats, whereas the RPP polled only 28.7% of the vote and won 134 seats and the smaller rightist parties (the RPNP, the NP, and the NTP) together received 12.2% of the vote and 61 seats.[18] With a majority of seats under its control, the JP no longer needed to form a coalition government until the next elections, scheduled for four years later, in 1969.

In the general elections of October 1969, the JP retained its majority, with 256 seats in the National Assembly. Despite its dominant position in the Assembly, the Demirel Government faced difficulties in carrying through some of the policies it had formulated during the previous four years. Internal party strife intensified and led to splits within the major parties as the economic situation worsened and gave rise to widespread social unrest.

To counteract the growing tide of social consciousness among the working people and progressive forces, and to channel their frustration into electoral politics, the RPP had, since the mid-1960s, begun to promote a 'left-of-centre' image under its Secretary-General, Bulent Ecevit. While this tactical departure prompted the party's right wing to break off in 1967 to form the Reliance Party (RP – *Guven Partisi*), it was able for a short time to dampen mass discontent against the prevailing order.

The RPNP had since the mid-1960s come under the control of Turkes and his fascist associates; and by 1969, it had changed its name to Nationalist Action Party (NAP – *Milli Hareket Partisi*). In early 1970 another right-wing party came into being called the National Order Party (NOP – *Milli Nizam Partisi*). It was founded by Necmettin Erbakan and advocated a return to Islamic fundamentalism, though its class basis was the Anatolian petty bourgeoisie. Also in 1970, a split occurred within the Justice Party. A section made up of large landowners broke away and formed themselves into the Democratic Party (DP – *Demokratik Parti*). This split, as it turned out, worked to the advantage of the comprador forces within the party, as they were now able to consolidate their control over the JP in the years following 1970.

These developments occurred in response to the growing strength of the working class and progressive forces in the country in the late 1960s, at a time when the economy was in profound crisis. The repressive policies of the Demirel regime against the popular forces had indeed created a situation similar to that of the late 1950s, when the combination of events had given rise to an explosive situation. Now, as before, the only option left to the ruling classes was military intervention. On March 12, 1971, a 'memorandum' was issued by the High Command for Demirel's resignation: Demirel resigned and the military took power. Before going into the details of the 1971 intervention and subsequent developments, we must examine the underlying material conditions that led to the military intervention – the problems of the Turkish economy, the condition of the working class and the oppressed masses, and working-class struggles throughout the 1960s.

The Economy in Crisis

When the military commanders took power in 1960, the Turkish economy was in dire straits. Output was stagnant and there were high levels of inflation and unemployment; a sizeable trade deficit; a large and ever-increasing external debt; and an associated balance of payments crisis. The 1960 intervention, therefore, was in good part a reaction to the worsening economic situation and to the unrest that followed as a result. However, the generals who were in charge of the junta had no intention of effecting any long-term social transformations. Having kept the social and class structure of the country intact, the reforms proposed in the new Constitution were doomed to failure from the very start. The maintenance by the generals of the existing social order on behalf of the dominant classes, however, meant the continuation and eventual worsening of the general crisis in the economy throughout the 1960s.

Expansion of Foreign and Local Private Capital Continues

Despite lip service in the early 1960s to reforms that would strengthen the public sector through state planning, state enterprises continued to be handed over to the private sector, and the State Planning Organization (SPO) was turned into a supportive institution of local and foreign private capital.

Foreign investment in Turkey grew at a much more rapid pace in the 1960s than it had during the previous decade. 'In the years 1951–61 foreign capital entering Turkey had averaged about TL 12.2 million a year; between 1962 and April 1963 total foreign investment rose to TL 40.3 million, an increase of 229%. This trend continued for the rest of the decade and during the nine years 1960–8 foreign investment in Turkey amounted to TL 551,920,845.'[19] The profits transferred abroad by the foreign corporations between 1965 and August 1969 alone amounted to TL 232,598,315.[20]

The Five Year Plans, formulated by the state during the 1960s, were qualitatively different from those adopted during the 1930s. While in the 1930s planning and state investments played an important role in the development of a diversified national economy and worked to safeguard and advance the long-term interests of the national industrial bourgeoisie, by the 1950s and early 1960s the state sector had become an integral part of a dependent economy based on foreign and local comprador capital. Planning was reintroduced in the 1960s to work *within the framework of this dependent capitalist economy* rather than *against* it. Those who had hoped that the 1960 coup would mark a new beginning toward the fulfilment of Kemalist goals became frustrated and later resigned from their technocratic posts as the real purpose behind the generals' so-called 'reforms' became apparent.

Throughout the 1960s and beyond, state policies reflected the interests of foreign capital and of local landlord-comprador interests who had consolidated their economic and political power during the previous decade under the Bayar-Menderes regime. Thus denationalization of the Turkish economy continued unabated. Major state enterprises continued to be transferred to foreign and local private hands. And this process accelerated the expansion of foreign and local private capital. The most important of these transfers were in mining – especially chromium – iron and steel, manufacturing, and raw material processing. While in the 1930s the extraction of Turkey's mineral wealth had been monopolized exclusively by the state-owned Eti Bank, by the mid-1950s – and especially after 1960 – foreign and local private capital were allowed and encouraged to enter this field. Thus, the Divrigi Mines were transferred to the privately owned Turkish

Iron and Steel Corporation; 75% of Turkey's chromium mining was handed over to local and foreign private corporations; and the state-owned Karabuk iron and steel mill was transferred to the Turkish Iron and Steel Works.[21] In the rubber industry, 80% of production had come under the control of three foreign firms – Goodyear, Pirelli, and Royal Tyre; in oil, despite the challenge posed by the state-owned Turkish Petroleum Corporation (TPAO), three oil companies – Mobil Oil, Shell, and British Petroleum – continued their monopolistic control and made even more inroads into the Turkish oil industry. In other sectors of the economy, transnational conglomerates such as Unilever, Philips, Squibbs, Abbot and Pfizer made large profits during this period.[22]

The process of foreign penetration into Turkish industry in the 1960s was further accelerated through joint ventures with local private and state enterprises, as the neo-colonial collaborators in Ankara 'acceded to the demand that foreign capital in the mixed companies should be 60–70% and more, instead of the 49% stipulated by Turkish law.'[23] This meant a more thorough integration of a large section of the national industrial bourgeoisie into the dependent economy and a gradual transformation of a section of the traditional comprador bourgeoisie into a dependent industrial class with direct ties to metropolitan transnational monopolies. As a result, the Turkish economy had effectively been turned into an appendage of the metropolitan-controlled world capitalist economy. This led to numerous adverse consequences, the most important of which were the chronic deficits in the balance of trade and balance of payments.

The Balance of Payments Crisis

Ever since the dismantling of the state capitalist economy in the post-war period, Turkey had continuously registered trade deficits. These deficits were sizeable enough during the 1950s, but they became much worse in the 1960s. While Turkey's foreign trade deficit averaged 310 million T.L. annually during 1950–59,[24] and was 325 million T.L. in 1959, it reached 1.3 billion T.L. in 1960 – the year the DP regime was overthrown. The situation became worse in subsequent years when the deficit increased to 1.5 billion T.L. in 1961, 2.2 billion T.L. in 1962, and 2.9 billion T.L. in 1963 (see Table 25).

Between 1963 and 1969 the deficit fluctuated between 1.0 and 2.5 billion T.L., rising to 3.2 billion T.L. in 1970. The following year, when the second military intervention took place, Turkey registered a huge 7.3 billion T.L. deficit in foreign trade. These deficits were partially offset by the remittances of Turkish workers employed abroad, which averaged 883 million T.L. annually between 1964 and 1970.[25] Workers' remittances rose to 3.1 billion T.L. in 1970 and 7.1 billion T.L. in 1971,[26] and were just enough to cover nearly all of the trade deficits for these two years. However, as we shall see, dependence on workers' remittances from abroad to balance the yearly trade deficits was later to prove disastrous, as thousands of workers were sent home during the recessions in Europe in the mid- and, more severely so, the late

1970s. Meanwhile, however, these remittances constituted an important source of foreign exchange earnings and contributed to the increase in the gross domestic product. Despite this contribution, Turkey continued to experience balance of payments difficulties throughout the 1960s and into the 1970s.

Table 25
Turkish Foreign Trade, 1959–71 (in millions of T.L.).

Year	*Imports*	*Exports*	*Deficit (–) Surplus (+)*
1959	1,316.0	990.6	– 325.4
1960	4,213.7	2,886.6	– 1,327.1
1961	4,585.1	3,120.7	– 1,464.4
1962	5,599.8	3,430.8	– 2,169.0
1963	6,216.1	3,312.8	– 2,903.3
1964	4,878.0	3,696.9	– 1,181.1
1965	5,193.3	4,173.6	– 1,019.7
1966	6,521.9	4,414.6	– 2,107.3
1967	6,216.8	4,701.0	– 1,515.8
1968	6,934.0	4,467.8	– 2,466.2
1969	6,785.3	4,831.5	– 1,953.8
1970	9,598.1	6,407.7	– 3,190.4
1971	16,474.4	9,090.0	– 7,384.4

Source: United Nations, *Yearbook of International Trade Statistics, 1975*, (New York: United Nations, 1976), p. 975.

In fact, Turkey's balance of payments had been deteriorating ever since the mid-1950s, but after the 1960 coup it reached crisis proportions. While the deficit on current account had averaged US$60 million for the years 1957 and 1958, it reached US$117 million in 1960, US$123 nillion in 1961, US$235 million in 1962, and US$256 million in 1963.[27] The average annual deficit for the years 1961–70 came to US$180 million, and with amortization of public debt the total average annual deficit reached US$300 million during this period.[28] One of the major reasons for the steadily worsening deficit in the balance of payments was the drain on the budget caused by increased military spending. Allocations for defence expenditure, which totalled 1.9 billion T.L. in 1960 rose to 2.6 billion T.L. in 1962, 3.2 billion T.L. in 1964, 3.8 billion T.L. in 1966 and 4.4 billion T.L. in 1968 – an average of 24.4% of the budget during this period.[29]

The continued deficit in the balance of payments led to extensive borrowing from the imperialist states and 'international' banks. Most of the 'aid' was channelled through the Aid Consortium for Turkey, which had been set up by the United States and a dozen West European countries, and later joined by the World Bank. In all, US$2.1 billion was extended to Turkey during 1963–70.[30] This meant a further increase in Turkey's total external debt and debt service obligations. According to the government's own figures, Turkey's total external debt had reached 12.9 billion T.L. by 1965 and 18.4 billion T.L. by 1969.[31] Debt service payments totalled 318 million T.L. in 1959–60, 669 million T.L. in 1961–62, and 1.2 billion T.L. in 1963–64.[32] By the end of the decade these payments were running at over 2.4 billion T.L. annually.[33] This, in turn, further aggravated the deficit on the balance of payments and necessitated more borrowing, thus leading Turkey into perpetual debt bondage.

In short, by the end of the 1960s, the Turkish economy was in as critical a state as in the 1950s. Planning by the state was ineffectual as denationalization continued, and came to serve the interests of expanding foreign and local private capital. Deficits in trade, increased military spending and the resultant budget deficits led to a crisis in the balance of payments. This, in turn, led to more external borrowing, which exacerbated the problem of foreign debt and debt servicing. These problems, coupled with the worsening inflation and unemployment situation, to be discussed in the next section, led to a general crisis in the economy, which soon began to affect the condition of the working class and the broad masses of the working people.

The Condition of the Working Class

While the national economy was in general crisis during the 1960s, the imperialist-directed industrialization schemes of this period produced high rates of growth in the dependent, neo-colonial economy. Industrial production grew from 13 billion T.L. in 1962 to 31.2 billion T.L. in 1971 – a 140% increase in ten years.[34] Accompanying this growth was an increase in the size of the working class. While the number of workers in industry totalled 975,509 in 1960, it doubled to 1,918,601 by 1970.[35] The proportion of industrial workers in the total labour force grew from 7.5% in 1960 to 12.1% in 1970.[36] In all, there were 4,324,553 workers in Turkey in 1970, who together constituted 27.3% of the labour force.[37]

The industrialization drive of this period, dependent as it was on foreign capital and based on advanced technology imported from abroad, was unable to absorb the large migrant population of dispossessed peasant families. Also, increased mechanization in the agricultural sector, while increasing productivity and profits for the large landowners, continued to drive many small and middle peasants into bankruptcy and threw thousands of agricultural workers out of work. This worsened rural unemployment which had already reached critical proportions during the previous decade. The resulting massive migration to the cities of the rural unemployed and underemployed continued throughout the 1960s, and increased the rate of urban unemployment as well. Thus, by 1967 the total number of unemployed had reached 1,440,000; i.e. 11% of the labour force.[38]

The condition of workers who had obtained employment on a regular basis also hardly improved during the 1960s, for their wages remained extremely low, despite increases from year to year. What little increases they won through persistent struggle were practically wiped out by spiralling inflation (see Table 26).

Table 26
Cost of Living Index, Ankara and Istanbul, 1960–71 (1960 = 100)*

Year	*Ankara*	*Istanbul*	*Average*
1960	100.0	100.0	100.0
1961	100.8	103.8	102.3
1962	105.3	107.4	106.3
1963	112.2	115.0	113.6
1964	115.1	118.0	116.5
1965	122.7	123.2	122.9
1966	129.5	133.1	131.3
1967	137.8	152.6	145.2
1968	143.5	162.0	152.7
1969	151.6	169.8	160.7
1970	169.4	183.3	176.3
1971	206.4	218.1	212.2

* The 1938 = 100 index adjusted to 1960 = 100.
Source: State Institute of Statistics, *Turkiye'de Toplumsal ve Ekonomik Gelismenin 50 Yili,* p. 367; my own computations added.

Average daily real wages of workers in industry increased slightly during the first half of the 1960s (due primarily to the relatively low rate of inflation during this period) but, except for 1967–69, stagnated or *declined* during the latter half of the decade. Overall, the average annual increase in real wages for workers in industry during the eleven-year period, 1961–71, amounted to 2.8% (see Table 27). Moreover, if we take into consideration the fact that the wage levels indicated in Table 27 are for insured workers only, include salaried employees, and do not take into account taxes, we can conclude that the average wages of workers in industry during this period were *much lower* than those indicated in the available data. Thus, while average daily gross wages of insured workers in industry during 1963–68 amounted to 22.66 T.L., the official minimum wage averaged 11.33 T.L. during the same period – exactly half as much. For a basic diet, the minimum daily expenditure on food for a five-member worker's family was 25.70 T.L. in 1966.[39] So the average daily gross wages of an insured industrial worker that year (23.74 T.L.) could not even meet the family's minimum nutritional requirements, let alone provide shelter and clothing, meet transportation expenses, and pay taxes! When we take into account the extremely low wages of agricultural workers (who do not have social

Table 27
Average Daily Wages* and Indices of Money Wages and Real Wages** by Major Sector, 1960–71***

Year	Wages	*Turkish Lira (TL)/Index (I)*	*Manufac-turing*	*Mining & Quarrying*	*Constr-uction*	*Transport, Storage & Communi cations*	*Average (all in-dustry)*
	Money Wages	TL	14.11	11.12	15.35	16.38	14.24
1960		I	100	100	100	100	100
	Real Wages	I	100	100	100	100	100
	Money Wages	TL	14.88	11.43	16.83	18.99	15.53
1961		I	105	103	110	116	109
	Real Wages	I	103	101	107	113	106
	Money Wages	TL	15.73	13.35	16.94	19.42	16.36
1962		I	111	120	110	118	115
	Real Wages	I	104	113	103	111	108
	Money Wages	TL	17.21	14.30	18.61	20.80	17.73
1963		I	122	128	121	127	124
	Real Wages	I	107	113	106	112	109
	Money Wages	TL	17.73	15.64	19.62	21.88	18.72
1964		I	126	141	128	133	131
	Real Wages	I	108	121	110	114	112
	Money Wages	TL	20.66	17.00	21.33	23.79	20.69
1965		I	146	153	139	145	145
	Real Wages	I	119	124	113	118	118
	Money Wages	TL	22.66	21.39	22.43	28.49	23.74

Year	*Wages*	*Turkish Lira (TL) Index (I)*	*Manufacturing*	*Mining & Quarrying*	*Construction*	*Transport Storage & Communications*	*Average (all industry)*
1966		I	160	192	146	174	167
	Real Wages	I	122	146	111	132	128
	Money Wages	TL	24.75	22.33	27.09	31.56	26.43
1967		I	175	201	176	193	186
	Real Wages	I	120	138	121	133	128
	Money Wages	TL	27.07	24.78	29.03	33.79	28.67
1968		I	192	223	189	206	201
	Real Wages	I	126	146	124	135	132
	Money Wages	TL	31.80	26.36	32.15	38.92	32.31
1969		I	225	237	209	238	227
	Real Wages	I	140	147	130	148	141
	Money Wages	TL	35.72	29.12	33.72	40.49	34.76
1970		I	253	262	220	247	244
	Real Wages	I	143	149	125	140	138
	Money Wages	TL	40.74	35.17	38.25	46.61	40.19
1971		I	289	316	249	284	282
	Real Wages	I	136	149	117	134	133
Average Annual Increase in Real Wages (1961–71)			*+ 2.9%*	*+ 3.9%*	*+ 1.5%*	*+ 2.8%*	*+ 2.8%*

* Including Salaries.

** Real wage indices were obtained by dividing money wage indices (derived from ILO data given in T.L.) by cost of living indices averaged for Ankara and Istanbul as provided in Table 26.

*** All wages and wage indices, including real wage indices, are based on *gross* wages, i.e., wages before the deduction of taxes and social security contributions.

Source: International Labour Organization, *Yearbook of Labour Statistics, 1970* (Geneva, International Labour Office, 1970), Tables 20–22; pp. 647, 653, 658; *1978,* Tables 17–20; pp. 511, 529, 535, 542; my own computations added.

security rights), those employed in the service sector, and other uninsured and non-unionized workers, the overall average wages of workers in Turkey drop even further.[40] This means that in the 1960s the wages of workers in Turkey, as a whole, were *well below the level of subsistence,* or the required minimum necessary to secure the healthy reproduction of the working class.

While hundreds of thousands of workers in Turkey lived on the brink of starvation in mud shacks, a handful of foreign and local capitalists fattened themselves and their bank accounts at the expense of the workers. The mass of surplus value extracted from workers in the manufacturing sector alone grew from 4,001,993,000 T.L. in 1963 to 14,219,800,000 T.L. in 1968, an increase of 225%.[41] This was accomplished through the super-exploitation of labour, the rate of exploitation increasing from 337% in 1963 to 443% in 1968.[42]

In the face of this naked capitalist assault, which threatened the very survival of the working class, the workers did not remain idle. In fact, the 1960s was a decade of intense struggle: hundreds of thousands of workers were mobilized in trade unions and party organizations and there were several hundred successful strikes and demonstrations.

Organized Labour and Class Struggle

The process of industrialization effected under the auspices of foreign and local comprador capital during the 1950s had led to an expansion in the size of the working class and, objectively, prepared the ground for the development of the labour movement through unionization. But the domination of yellow trade unions, organized under the class-collaborationist Confederation of Turkish Trade Unions, *Turk-Is,* blocked and misdirected working-class struggles, channelling them into narrow economic concerns. Connected with the North American AFL-CIO and the CIA,[43] *Turk Is* had no real intention of struggling to secure even the most elementary of workers' rights – the right to strike. By the end of the 1950s, the blatantly reactionary policies of the Menderes regime had provided an opening for rank-and-file workers to begin to take matters into their own hands. The role of the workers in the activities which led to the downfall of the Menderes regime was sufficiently important to win them concessions such as the right to strike from the military commanders who overthrew Menderes in 1960. These concessions were written into the new Constitution. Utilizing their newly won rights, workers began to form many new trade unions and pressed their demands for the implementation of the reforms promised under the new Constitution. Two hundred new trade unions were formed in the early 1960s, bringing the total number of unions to 409 by 1966 and to 717 by 1970.[44] And, while union membership stood at 250,000 in 1959, it increased to 300,000 in 1963 and to 600,000 in 1965.[45]

A new stage in the development of the workers' movement began at the end of 1961, when 200,000 workers demonstrated in Istanbul, demanding an end to unemployment, the right to strike, and a law on collective bargaining. This demonstration, which included union delegates from 29 provinces, was the biggest ever in the 40-year history of the Republic. In 1962, while strikes were still banned, a major demonstration was again organized by the Building Workers Union in Ankara and thousands of workers marched from Ulus Square to the Grand National Assembly, protesting against unemployment, the ban on strikes, and related issues. In the ensuing clashes with the police, 300 workers were arrested. Strikes and demonstrations continued to gather momentum during this period. Two notable examples were the protest meeting against the American Morrison-Knudsen Company in Eregli, in which representatives of 210 trade unions took part, and the five-week strike at the Turkish-American owned Kavel cable factory in Istanbul.[46] In all, during the period 1961–63, there were more than 40 strikes and many more demonstrations.

There was greater scope for strikes and demonstrations following the passage in 1963 of the law legalizing the right to strike in sectors of the economy that did not 'jeopardize national security'. Between 1963 and 1966 83 strikes took place, most of them over unemployment and low wages. Despite the economic focus of these strikes, many of them – especially those involving foreign companies – became *political* and acquired an anti-imperialist character. This was clearly the case during the protest meeting against the American Morrison-Knudsen Company, when protesting workers declared: 'If foreign companies do not comply with our warnings, they must immediately leave our land.'[47] Similar warnings were given to the British and American oil companies in 1963, by the workers on strike at the ATAS refinery in Mersin.[48]

Workers' struggles grew and intensified in the latter half of the 1960s as the level of organization and consciousness of the working class reached new heights. In 1965, more than 6,000 miners went on strike and staged demonstrations in Zonguldak. The police and naval forces were sent in, and the city was surrounded by the Army. Clashes between the workers and the armed forces left two workers dead and numerous others injured.[49] In 1966, textile workers in Izmir went on strike for two months. And, during the demonstrations that followed, the police opened fire, killing two workers. Bloody clashes between the workers and the police continued in other strikes and demonstrations throughout Turkey during this period and showed the growing strength of the workers' movement, which was gaining momentum despite the assaults unleashed against it by the state. These developments opened the way to solidarity between workers in different sectors of the economy and between workers and students. The refusal of the Confederation of Turkish Trade Unions, *Turk-Is,* to support the Zonguldak strike prompted seven unions to leave *Turk-Is* and establish a separate federation.[50] And messages of solidarity were sent to the striking miners in Zonguldak by the Turkish National Student Association and the National Student Federation of Turkey. With the backing of their organizations, the students, together with other workers, marched in Ankara in support of the striking miners.[51]

Battling against the yellow trade unionism of *Turk-Is* in the 1960s were a number of independent unions and workers' organizations. Among these were the Istanbul Trade Union Association, the Mine Workers Union, and the Workers Party of Turkey (WPT). Founded in 1961 by 12 independent trade unionists, the WPT played an important role in the above-mentioned strikes and demonstrations and, through its links with numerous independent unions, helped elevate these struggles to a more political level. The number of unions that were tied to or gave support to the party increased throughout the 1960s and included among others the Mine Workers Union, the Press Technicians Union, the Tyre Workers Union, the Food Workers Union, and the Chemical Workers Union.[52] The WPT-initiated fight against yellow trade unionism in general, and *Turk-Is* in particular, resulted in victory with the establishment in 1967 of the Confederation of Revolutionary Trade Unions (*Devrimci Isci Sendikalari Konfederasyonu* or DISK) by a group of unions which withdrew from *Turk-Is*.

Founded by the above-mentioned unions associated with the WPT, DISK became a rallying point for class-conscious workers and trade unionists and progressive organizations throughout Turkey. Its establishment as a politically mature workers' organization signalled the beginning of a new stage in the labour movement and raised the class struggle to a new plane.

Aided by these developments, and by the changing context of labour struggles following the founding of DISK, workers' militancy increased to a point where massive strikes, demonstrations, and factory occupations became common occurrences by the end of the decade. In 1968, 1,800 workers at the Derby rubber factory carried out the first factory occupation in Turkey.[53] Strike activity intensified between 1968 and 1970, and the number of industrial strikes increased from 54 in 1968 to 81 in 1969 and to 112 in 1970.[54] The number of workers involved in these strikes increased from 5,259 in 1968 to 15,134 in 1969 and to 21,150 in 1970.[55] Through these struggles, workers were able to strengthen their ranks and improve their relative position at the end of the 1960s. As a result, the rate of exploitation fell from 443% in 1968 to 331% in 1970.[56]

In the meantime, the general economic situation continued to worsen as the rate of inflation and unemployment reached new levels, the deficit in the balance of trade and the balance of payments drained the country's exchange earnings and increased its external debt, and the industrial growth rate dropped from 12% in 1965–69 to 1.5% in 1970.[57]

The rapidly deteriorating situation in 1970 reminded many of the developments that had led to the overthrow of the Menderes regime a decade earlier, and gave rise to concern about renewed military intervention. But the workers were not prepared to become victims of the ailing capitalist economy in order to save the bosses' system. Thus, on June 15–16, 1970, more than 100,000 workers in Istanbul and Kocaeli stopped work in 135 factories, protesting at an attempt to amend the law governing unions, which was intended to weaken the trade union movement. In the demonstrations that followed, bloody clashes took place between the workers, the Army, and police throughout Istanbul. The right-wing government of Demirel was able to control the situation only by declaring martial law.[58] Not long after these events the military moved in again to intervene directly and prevent a mass insurrection.

References

1. On various aspects of these factions, see E.K. Trimberger, *Revolution from Above: Military Bureaucrats and Development in Japan, Turkey, Egypt, and Peru,* (New Brunswick, NJ: Transaction Books, 1978), pp. 131–3; F. Ahmad, *The Turkish Experiment,* pp. 161–8; J. Landau, *Radical Politics in Modern Turkey,* pp. 11–14, 206–32.
2. F. Ahmad, *The Turkish Experiment, op. cit.,* pp. 157–8.
3. K. Karpat, 'The Military and Politics in Turkey, 1960–64: A Socio-Cultural Analysis of a Revolution', *American Historical Review,* Vol. 75, No. 6 (October 1970), p. 1666.
4. *Ibid.* Also see E. Ozbudun, *The Role of the Military in Recent Turkish Politics,* (Cambridge, Mass.: Harvard University, Centre for International Affairs, 1966), p. 19.
5. For, as Trimberger points out, 'Representatives of the highest military elites [who] joined and supported . . . the 1960 coup in Turkey . . . never shared the ideals which motivated the junior officers. It was these senior officers who repressed the young fascists in order to retain the conservative coalition between bureaucrats and the landlord and capitalist classes . . . Such officers intervened in politics to uphold the *status quo* through minor reform'. E.K. Trimberger, *op. cit.,* p. 132.
6. As pointed out earlier, after a year-long investigation of their crimes, most were found guilty and given various sentences, including fifteen death sentences of which three were carried out.
7. W. Weiker, *The Turkish Revolution, 1960–1961* (Washington D.C.: The Brookings Institution, 1963), p. 131.
8. Y. Sertel, *Turkiye'de Ilerici Akimlar,* pp. 118–31.
9. Y. Demir, 'Turkey in the Grip of Reaction', *World Marxist Review,* Vol. 6, No. 11 (November 1963), pp. 24–5.
10. W. Weiker, *op. cit.,* p. 163.
11. F. Ahmad, *The Turkish Experiment, op. cit.,* pp. 212–13.
12. *Ibid.,* p. 217. Those who resigned included the Under-Secretary and principal adviser at the SPO, Osman Nuri Torun; Head of the Office of Economic Affairs, Atilla Karaosmanoglu; Head of the Office of Social Affairs, Nejat Erder; and Head of the Office for Co-ordination, Ayhan Cilingiroglu. *Ibid.,* p. 229, f. 23.
13. These included the editor of the party paper *Ulus,* the renowned novelist Yakup Kadri Karaosmanoglu; a long-time member of the RPP, Falih Rifki Atay; and other committed Kemalists.
14. *Ibid.,* p. 219.

15. *Ibid.*, p. 220.
16. *Ibid.*, p. 225.
17. On this point, see the Turkish press: *Cumhuriyet*, Sept. 13 and Oct. 9, 1965; *Akis*, Oct. 16, 1965; *Yon*, Oct. 15, 1965.
18. F. Ahmad, *The Turkish Experiment op. cit.*, pp. 191–2.
19. *Ibid.*, p. 279.
20. *Ibid.*, p. 286, f.35.
21. Y. Sertel, *op. cit.*, p. 157.
22. *Ibid.*, pp. 161–7.
23. Y. Demir, *op. cit.*, p. 21.
24. IBRD, (World Bank), (1975) *Turkey: Prospects and Problems of an Expanding Economy*, (Washington, DC: World Bank, 1975), p. 125.
25. Turkish workers went abroad, mainly to West Germany but also to other European countries, starting in 1964. Their remittances for the years 1964–70 were, on the basis of the prevailing exchange rate of US$1 = 9 T.L.,as follows: 180 million T.L. in 1964; 720 million T.L. in 1965; 1.1 billion T.L. in 1966; 900 million T.L. in 1967; 1.1 billion T.L. in 1968; and 1.3 billion T.L. in 1969. *Ibid.*, p. 125.
26. Organization for Economic Co-operation and Development (OECD), *Turkey*, (Paris: OECD, 1978), p. 55. The US $ conversion is based on the official exchange rate of US$1 = 9 T.L. prior to August 9, 1970, and US$1 = 15 T.L. during the period August 9, 1970, to December 22, 1971. World Bank, *Turkey*, p. iii.
27. Z.Y. Hershlag, *Turkey*, p. 367.
28. World Bank, (1975) *op. cit.*, p. 129.
29. US Agency for International Development, *Economic and Social Indicators – Turkey*, (Ankara: USAID, 1969), pp. 46–7. To put defence spending in perspective, it should be pointed out that while in 1963 the Ministry of National Defence was allotted 2.9 billion T.L., the Ministry of Agriculture received only 440 million T.L. and the Ministry of Industry a mere 190 million T.L.
30. Including US$1.3 billion of Consortium credits and US$786 million of project credits. See A.O. Krueger, *Turkey*, p. 134.
31. State Institute of Statistics, *Turkiye Istatistik Yilligi, 1971*, (Statistical Yearbook of Turkey, 1971), (Ankara: Devlet Istatistik Enstitusu Matbaasi, 1973), p. 377. And, if we add to these figures the internal public debt of 22.6 billion T.L. in 1969, the total debt for 1969 comes to 41 billion T.L. *Ibid.*, p. 376.
32. Z.Y. Hershlag, *op. cit.*, pp. 21–2.
33. A.O. Krueger, *op. cit.*, p. 134. The US$205 million figure given by Krueger for 1970 is converted into Turkish currency, based on the prevailing exchange rate given in Reference 26 above.
34. F. Ahmad, *The Turkish Experiment, op. cit.*, p. 280. Similarly, the process of capitalist transformation of the agrarian sector continued with full speed, such that the area of land cultivated by machine increased from 19% in 1960 to 30% in 1969, while the number of tractors used increased from 50,844 in 1963 to nearly 100,000 in 1969. *Ibid.*, p. 283; Z.Y. Hershlag, *op. cit.*, p. 356; Y. Sertel, *op. cit.*, pp. 79–80.
35. International Labour Organization, *Yearbook of Labour Statistics, 1965*, (Geneva: ILO, 1966), Table 2A, pp. 124–5; State Institute of Statistics,

Statistical Pocket Book of Turkey, 1974, (Ankara: S.I.S., 1975), Table 68, pp. 68–9; my own computations added.

36. *Ibid.*
37. *Ibid.*
38. OECD, *op. cit.*, p. 31.
39. The 25.70 T.L. minimum is based on a calculation of the required amounts of food items listed in Reference 40 in Chapter Five above, on the basis of prevailing prices in 1966. See State Institute of Statistics, *Statistical Yearbook of Turkey, 1971,* Table 401, p. 427.
40. Thus, as Y. Demir points out, 'Monthly wages in the textile industry average 300 lire, but the official minimum for a family of four is 2,300 lire a month. Some categories of workers in the mining industry earn a bare 160 lire a month, working 14–16 hours a day, but a doctor's fee for a visit is 30–50 lire.' Y. Demir, 'Turkey in the Grip of Reaction', p. 22.
41. R. Yurukoglu, *Turkey – Weak Link of Imperialism,* p. 154.
42. *Ibid.*, p. 59. With the rise in the rate of exploitation, there occurred a large increase in the number of accidents at work: from 63,014 in 1960 to 92,961 in 1965 to 144,731 in 1970. *Ibid.*, p. 75.
43. On this point, see *The Washington Post* (May 23, 1966), and John Kelly, 'CIA and Labour in Turkey', *Counter Spy,* Vol. 4., No. 2 (Spring 1980).
44. State Institute of Statistics, *Statistical Yearbook of Turkey, 1971,* p. 169.
45. Y. Sertel, *op. cit.*, p. 144.
46. Y. Demir, *op. cit.*, p. 24.
47. Y. Sertel, *op. cit.*, p. 142.
48. *Ibid.*, pp. 142–3.
49. *Ibid.*, p. 143.
50. *Ibid.*, p. 144.
51. *Ibid.*
52. *Ibid.*, p. 147.
53. R. Yurukoglu, *op. cit.*, p. 87.
54. International Labour Organization, *Yearbook of Labour Statistics, 1977,* (Geneva: ILO, 1977), Table 27, p. 850.
55. *Ibid.*
56. R. Yurukoglu, *op. cit.*, p. 59.
57. State Institute of Statistics, *Turkiye'nin Milli Geliri, 1962–1977,* ('Turkey's National Income, 1962–1977'), (Ankara: Devlet Istatistik Enstitusu Matbaasi, 1978).
58. R. Yurukoglu, *op. cit.*, p. 87. Also, see T. Arinir and S. Ozturk, *Isci Sinifi, Sendikalar ve 15/16 Haziran* ('The Working Class, Trade Unions and June 15/16'), (Istanbul: Sorun Yayinlari, 1976).

7. The Neo-colonial Crisis and the Revolutionary Situation, 1971-79

The economic and social problems of the late 1960s and early 1970s, which led to a renewed crisis of the state, in effect constituted a new phase in the prolonged crisis of the neo-colonial system installed in Turkey in the early 1950s and reinforced following the military coup in 1960. With the increase in the level and intensity of the urban class struggle during the 1960s, and especially towards the end of the decade, the working class and the popular forces came to threaten openly the rule of the neo-colonial state with massive social insurrection.[1] Seeing its interests threatened by the developing revolutionary situation, the Turkish bourgeoisie – acting with the support and backing of imperialism – moved to 'halt' and 'reverse' this process through renewed military intervention.

The 1971 Military Intervention

On March 12, 1971 the generals moved in to take full control of the state apparatus. Their purpose was to retain power in the hands of the ruling classes in a period of economic and political crisis and social unrest that threatened the survival of the neo-colonial state.[2]

Following the military takeover, an 'above party' government was formed by a reactionary law professor, Nihat Erim, in late March. Erim's cabinet included, among others, Atilla Karaosmanoglu of the World Bank, Ihsan Topaloglu, ex-director of the Turkish Petroleum Company, Sait Naci Ergin, a representative of the bankers, and Ferit Melen of the reactionary Reliance Party. Shortly after the formation of the government, martial law was declared on April 26 in eleven strategic provinces, including the country's eight most industrialized provinces, where DISK was strongest, and three rural provinces with a large Kurdish population.[3] All strikes and demonstrations were outlawed, left-wing political organizations and publications were banned, liberal and progressive newspapers were closed down, and journalists associated with them were prosecuted, and thousands of trade unionists, students, and teachers were detained, while all students and teachers unions were banned and their leaders were imprisoned.[4]

In an attempt to silence opposition and consolidate military rule, a large number of constitutional amendments were passed to restrict or abolish basic rights, such as the freedom of speech and of assembly and the right to form trade unions.

In early 1972 a new phase of military repression began when in an operation code-named *Tornado I,* over 80,000 troops and police terrorized Istanbul, searching more than half a million houses, offices and workshops.[5] Thousands of progressive students, teachers, lawyers, journalists, and trade unionists were arrested, imprisoned, and tortured during this period.[6] Despite the brutal methods and atrocities carried out by the military regime against the opposition forces, the Government was unable to silence the people and halt their struggle against the military dictatorship. Under the guise of preparing the nation for elections, the generals succeeded in passing a series of constitutional amendments to ensure the continuation of a repressive regime behind the facade of constitutionality.

Coalition Governments of the 1970s

Between 1973 and 1979 Turkey lived through a period of unstable and precarious coalition governments which fell one after another. These governments were led alternately by the reactionary Justice Party (JP) and the 'social democratic' Republican People's Party (RPP),[7] based on an alliance with an assortment of right-wing parties. In early 1974 the RPP, led by Bulent Ecevit, formed a coalition government with the reactionary Islamist National Salvation Party (NSP). But this unstable coalition lasted only until September of that year. The coalition government that emerged in the subsequent period was a so-called Nationalist Front. This reactionary fascist coalition was formed by an alliance of four right-wing parties – the JP, NSP, RRP (Republican Reliance Party), and NAP (Nationalist Action Party) – under the leadership of Demirel. This coalition remained in power until the elections in June 1977. In the intervening period the state was ransacked by the reactionaries. The JP had a free hand in utilizing the state sector to expand the interests of the compradors, while the NAP fascists obtained key positions within the government apparatus, especially inside the secret service and the police and armed forces. The economic policies of the Nationalist Front Government, which were designed to serve the short-term profit interests of the comprador capitalists, led Turkey into a deeper economic crisis which was to bring the country to the brink of bankruptcy, as we shall see shortly.

The effects of the government's reactionary policies began to be felt by 1977, and conflicts developed within and between the Nationalist Front parties over these policies. Thus, the second Nationalist Front Government, which came to power following the June 1977 elections, survived only until the end of the year. In January 1978, Ecevit, with support from Independents, formed a new, RPP-led government.[8] While this meant the end of right-wing coalition governments for the time being, it did not signal a major reversal of trends in the economy. The economic situation worsened throughout 1978 and 1979, and when in October 1979 the RPP failed to secure the necessary seats in parliamentary by-elections, which meant the loss of its parliamentary majority, Ecevit and his cabinet promptly resigned.[9] Once again Demirel was asked to form a government, and by the closing months of 1979 a JP-led right-wing government had been formed, thus placing Turkey on the path of yet another reactionary course.

In all, the coalition governments formed during the period 1973–79 numbered 13, and none of them was able to resolve the mounting economic problems which had brought Turkey to the brink of a major depression. These continued crises in the economy dragged the country from one ruling-class government coalition to another, and led to increased unrest and militancy among the masses, which, as on two previous occasions, reached explosive proportions by the end of the 1970s. Before examining the class struggles of this period, it is worthwhile taking a closer look at the faltering economic situation in Turkey in the 1970s.

The Economic Crisis Persists

The 1971 military intervention had taken place in response to the faltering economy and the mass strikes and demonstrations which followed as a result in the early 1970s. But the generals had an added interest in preserving the neo-colonial *status quo* and repressing brutally the people's forces: since the early 1960s, the armed forces had themselves, through the establishment of the Army Mutual Assistance Association (*Ordu Yardimlasma Kurumu* – OYAK), emerged as one of the largest industrial and commercial interests in Turkey, and in this way had become an integral part of the neo-colonial economy.[10] By the early 1970s OYAK had come to acquire controlling interests in the Turkish Automotive Industry, which assembles International Harvester trucks and tractors; an insurance company; a food canning firm; and a cement plant.[11] It also held 42% of the shares of Renault's Turkish subsidiary OYAK-Renault, 20% of the Petkim Petrochemical plant, 8% of the state-owned Turkish Petroleum Corporation, and 7% of the Turkish subsidiary of the Goodyear Tyre Company, among others.[12] Thus, while it had started with an initial investment of 8.6 million T.L., by 1970 its investments had grown to 502 million T.L., and in all, its assets in 1972 totalled US$300 million.[13]

Given its important position in the economy, alongside the rising Turkish monopoly bourgeoisie, the military had a substantial stake in the maintenance of economic and social stability. But could this be achieved within the framework of a neo-colonial economy dependent on foreign capital? The answer was becoming increasingly clear as the economy continued to deteriorate and plunged into a deeper crisis by the mid-1970s.

The Balance of Payments Crisis

Throughout the 1970s Turkey continued to register a deficit in its external trade. Imports grew at a rapid pace while exports lagged far behind. The net effect of this imbalance was a steady deterioration in the country's balance of trade. In 1970 the deficit in foreign trade was 3.2 billion T.L., and it increased to 7.4 billion T.L. after the military intervention in 1971. By 1974 it was over 31 billion T.L. With a continued increase in imports and a drop in the value of exports the following year, the deficit reached 47.5 billion T.L. in 1975. And by 1977 it registered a record 71.7 billion T.L.! (see Table 28).

Table 28
Turkish Foreign Trade, 1970–77 (in millions of T.L.)

Year	*Imports*	*Exports*	*Deficit (–) Surplus (+)*
1970	9,598.1	6,407.7	– 3,190.4
1971	16,474.4	9,090.0	– 7,384.4
1972	21,564.1	11,875.9	– 9,688.2
1973	29,263.3	18,037.4	– 11,225.9
1974	52,310.9	21,197.3	– 31,113.6
1975	67,553.6	20,075.1	– 47,478.5
1976	80,753.1	30,775.5	– 49,977.6
1977	103,031.0	31,338.5	– 71,692.5

Source: United Nations, *Yearbook of International Trade Statistics, 1977*, (New York: United Nations, 1978), p. 923.

Workers' remittances from abroad partially offset the deficit in the early 1970s when these increased from US$471 million in 1971 to US$1.4 billion in 1974.[14] But when in the mid-1970s European firms began to cut back on foreign labour because of the recession and sent thousands of workers home, there occurred a sharp reduction in the volume of these remittances. So the amount sent home by Turkish workers from abroad fell to $982 million in 1976 and remained at that level in 1977 and 1978.[15]

Foreign borrowing allowed the government to cover the deficit in the short run, but the added debt and debt-servicing obligations further aggravated Turkey's balance of payments crisis. The deficit on current account increased from US$122 million in 1971 to US$720 million in 1974, and to US$3.4 billion in 1977.[16] And this does not include the amortization of public debt, which totalled US$574 million in 1977 alone – with US$360 million of it going as interest payments on previous debt.[17]

Mounting Foreign Debt: The Economy Mortgaged to Western Banks

Turkey's total foreign debt was US$2.2 billion in 1970, and it had increased to US$3.5 billion by 1975. But, by the end of 1977 it had reached US$12.5 billion![18] A year later, in 1978, it had increased further to US$13.5 billion,[19] and in 1979 to over US$15 billion. Faced with this crisis, Turkey's creditors, among whom are the so-called 'international' financial agencies and more than 250 private Western banks, began to stage a 'rescue operation' in 1979. Among the conditions imposed on Turkey by the International Monetary Fund (IMF) for the extension of further credit were: deceleration of economic growth (which had already fallen from 7% per year prior to 1976 to about 2% in 1978); a wage freeze; a 20–30% devaluation of the Turkish lira already devalued on 15 occasions between 1972 and 1977!); a further increase in consumer prices; and large allocations to the private sector from the state budget – a budget already running a deficit of several billion dollars.[20] To carry out the 'rescue operation' – in concert with the above IMF 'austerity package' – a consortium of seven foreign banks began work in early 1979 on the rescheduling and reordering of Turkey's massive foreign debts, which the *Financial Times* called 'one of the largest such operations in financial history, involving some 6 billion US dollars'.[21]

Figure 2, Turkish Foreign Trade, 1970–77

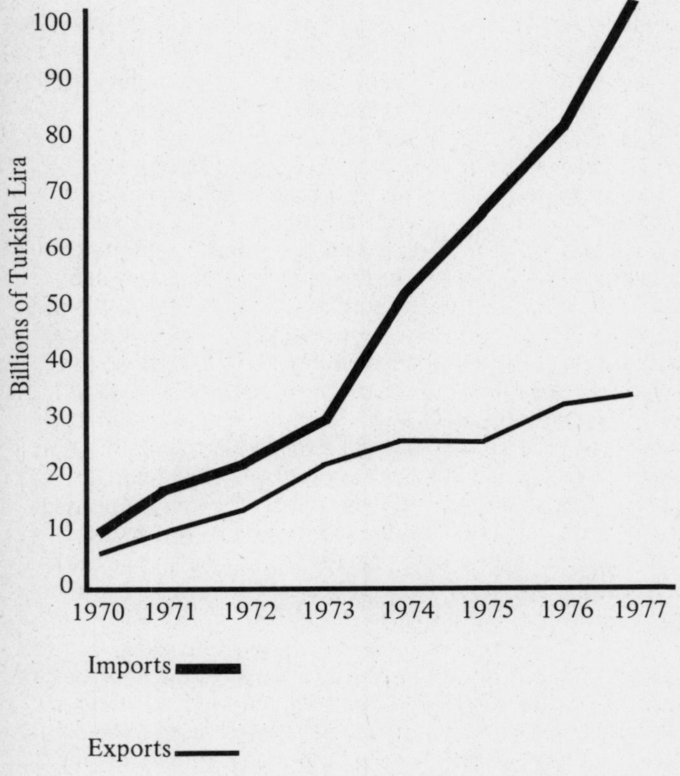

Source: United Nations, *Yearbook of International Trade Statistics, 1977*, (New York: United Nations, 1978), p. 923.

The real effects of this latest round of imperialist assault on the working people of Turkey – carried out via the agents of imperialism, the collaborating Turkish bourgeoisie – have already begun to be felt. The lira has been devalued several times in 1979–80, on one occasion by 48%;[22] the rate of inflation reached 100% in 1979; the real wages of workers are rapidly declining; the rate of growth of the gross national product is now *zero;* 50% of industrial plant capacity is lying idle; the unemployment rate is 20% and rising; and widespread shortages of basic commodities, electricity cuts on a daily basis, scarcity of heating fuel, medicines, and other necessities have created an atmosphere of panic among the population.[23]

In the midst of this grim economic situation in Turkey, a new round of talks began in late 1979 regarding the ramifications of Turkey's longstanding application to join the European Economic Community (EEC) as a 'way out' of its underdeveloped and crisis-ridden position in the world economy. Although the prospect of Turkish membership of the EEC is at this point far from certain, the consequences of such membership on the Turkish economy would certainly be grave. Turkish entry into the Common Market would be of decisive advantage to European capital and, more broadly, to global transnational monopolies. It would mean to them an opportunity for expanded foreign investments without any restrictions; direct access to abundant cheap labour; access to a steady supply of much-needed oil and other raw materials; lifting of tariff barriers and other import restrictions to capture a greater share of the local market; further monopolization of the local economy, especially in industry; the continuation of Turkish reintegration into the world economy, now under European sponsorship; and providing the needed political stability in Turkey so that it may fulfil its assigned functions in accordance with the interests of foreign capital and its reactionary internal class allies. In contrast to these benefits accruing to foreign and local ruling classes, Turkey's prospective membership in the EEC would have major consequences on the less privileged classes, as well as on the national economy as a whole. It would force more small farmers and businesses into bankruptcy, and hence cause the further depopulation of the countryside and overpopulation of cities with already large unemployed and underemployed populations; worsen inflation through foreign monopoly control over prices of basic commodities, and, with the suppression of wages, lower the real income of workers, and hence lower their living standards; put major demands on workers, such as lower pay increases, no-strike clauses, and other state-sanctioned controls, to encourage foreign investment; worsen the country's balance of trade and balance of payments, through increased imports and the lack of sufficient funds to pay for these, given the persistence of low foreign exchange earnings from underpriced export commodities; increase foreign debt and debt-servicing, as more loans would need to be issued by the EEC to 'overcome' these problems; continue its immense expenditures on the military, as the country's role and responsibilities in NATO expand in that region of the world; and in this way further increase its dependence on the West, preventing a break away from the Western capitalist orbit.[24]

In the present context, however, the economic and socio-political crises in which Turkey finds itself are so intense and explosive that, despite all the benefits European capital would draw from it, Turkish membership in the EEC is not viewed by the European parliament as an immediate prospect, at least for several more years. In the meantime, while it is in the interests of both US and European capital to put Turkey's financial house in order, through large amounts of external 'aid', the EEC has decided that the same functions can just as effectively be carried out by Turkey's western neighbour, Greece. Although the short-term financial remedies provided to it by the imperialist countries and agencies are intended to rescue Turkey from economic collapse and to prepare it for its future transition into the EEC, the situation of the working class has worsened, as more and more workers have become the victims of such continued imperialist schemes.

The Position of the Working Class

In 1970, there were a total of 4,324,533 wage workers in Turkey, accounting for 27.3% of the entire labour force.[25] Of this total, 1,918,601 (or 44.4%) were industrial workers.[26] By 1975, the size of the working class had increased by 29.7% over 1970, reaching 5,609,000 or 36% of the labour force.[27] In industry, it reached 2,309,000 or 14.8% of the total labour force.[28] With the growth in size of the working class during this period, there occurred a significant growth in the number of unionized workers. Union membership increased from 1,200,000 in 1971 to 2,000,000 in 1978, with DISK, the Confederation of Revolutionary Trade Unions, accounting for nearly one-half of the total. Union membership in Turkey in 1971 was 30% i.e. higher than in France (20%) and West Germany (25%).[29] It grew rapidly in subsequent years, reaching 42.8% of all wage-earners eligible to become members of trade unions in 1975.[30] This growth is a reflection of the increasing influence of DISK in the workers' movement.

The unionization drive of the late 1960s and early 1970s made possible the signing of better wage contracts. As a result, money wages showed a relative increase during this period (see Table 29).

Average daily money wages of insured workers in industry increased at an average annual rate of 12.5% between 1971 and 1978. But the increase in the cost of living during this period averaged 28.7% a year, reaching 40% at the end of 1977 and 90% in 1978 (see Table 30). And, in 1979, the rate of inflation was a record 100%![31]

This means that the nominal gains in money wages secured by workers in industry during the 1970s were practically wiped out by runaway inflation. Real wages declined in three of the seven years and, except in 1975–76, when the working class waged an all-out struggle and secured substantial gains, increased only slightly in the rest. The biggest drop in real wages came in 1978, when a fall of 22.8% was registered over the previous year.[32] Overall,

Table 29
Average Daily Wages* by Sector, 1971-78***

	1971			*1972*			*1973*			*1974*		
Sector	*Money Wages T.L.*	*I*	*Real** Wages I*	*Money Wages T.L.*	*I*	*Real Wages I*	*Money Wages T.L.*	*I*	*Real Wages I*	*Money Wages T.L.*	*I*	*Real Wages I*
Manufacturing	40.74	100	100	45.21	111	96	57.28	140	106	70.92	174	110
Mining and Quarrying	35.17	100	100	37.60	107	93	52.41	149	112	59.60	169	107
Construction	38.25	100	100	41.71	109	94	48.10	126	95	64.51	169	107
Transport, Storage and Communications	46.61	100	100	52.54	113	98	62.08	133	100	74.17	159	100
Average (all industry)	40.19	100	100	44.26	110	95	54.97	137	103	67.30	167	105

* Including salaries.

** Real wage indices were obtained by dividing money wage indices (derived from ILO data given in T.L.) by cost of living indices averaged for Ankara and Istanbul as provided in Table 30.

*** All wages and wage indices, including real wage indices, are based on *gross* wages, i.e. wages before the deduction of taxes and social security contributions.

Sector	1975 Money Wages T.L.	1975 I	1975 Real Wages I	1976 Money Wages T.L.	1976 I	1976 Real Wages I	1977 Money Wages T.L.	1977 I	1977 Real Wages I	1978 Money Wages T.L.	1978 I	1978 Real Wages I
Manufacturing	89.75	220	115	126.29	310	139	127.52	313	113	n.a.	n.a.	n.a.
Mining and Quarrying	90.19	256	134	112.10	319	143	144.57	411	148	n.a.	n.a.	n.a.
Construction	77.15	202	106	105.54	276	124	126.60	331	119	n.a.	n.a.	n.a.
Transport, Storage and Communications	120.15	258	135	117.44	252	113	165.30	355	128	n.a.	n.a.	n.a.
Average (all industry)	94.31	235	123	115.34	287	129	145.49	352	127	207.93	517	98

Source: International Labour Organization, *Yearbook of Labour Statistics, 1978*, (Geneva: International Labour Office, 1978) Table 17, 18, 19, 20; pp. 434, 529, 535, 542.

Table 30
Cost of Living Index, Ankara and Istanbul, 1971–78 (1971 = 100)*

Year	*Ankara*	*Annual Increase (%)*	*Istanbul*	*Annual Increase (%)*	*Average*	*Annual Increase (%)*
1971	100.0	–	100.0	–	100.0	–
1972	114.9	14.9	115.7	15.7	115.3	15.3
1973	133.1	15.8	131.9	14.0	132.5	14.9
1974	153.6	15.4	163.2	23.7	158.4	19.5
1975	182.9	19.1	197.8	21.2	190.4	20.2
1976	213.3	16.6	232.4	17.5	222.9	17.1
1977	261.3	22.5	292.4	25.8	276.9	24.2
1978	482.9	84.8	567.0	93.9	525.0	89.6

* The 1963 = 100 index, adjusted to 1971 = 100.
Source: Organization for Economic Co-operation and Development, *Turkey*, (Paris: OECD, 1978), p. 52; Turkiye Is Bankasi A.S., *Review of Economic Conditions, 1979,* No. 4 (Ankara, 1979), p. 28; my own computations added.

the average annual increase in real wages during 1971–78 was 0.4%.

When we examine the level of wages in relation to the ability of workers to purchase basic necessities, the picture becomes even clearer. In 1974, a five-member worker's family had to spend 78.50 T.L. per day on food alone,[33] but the average daily gross wage of an insured worker in industry was only 67.30 T.L. By 1978, 246.33 T.L. per day was needed for food alone, and, with inflation running at 100% in 1979, this figure had reached 493 T.L. a year later. Considering all the other expenses of a worker and his family, the *required* minimum daily wage – or the value of unskilled labour power – in 1979 was over 1,200 T.L.[34] Yet, the average daily gross wage in industry in 1978 was in fact only 207.93 T.L.! This means that in the 1970s, as in the 1950s and 1960s, the wages received by even the 'highest paid', insured workers were only a fraction of the required minimum wage and were not even enough to cover their families' nutritional requirements! Taking into account all the remaining, uninsured and non-unionized workers, it is clear that the level of wages of workers as a whole was *far below* the level of subsistence, with millions of workers threatened with malnutrition and wholesale starvation. It is no wonder that millions of workers have for decades been unable to move out of insanitary and totally inadequate shanty dwellings and obtain decent housing. In fact, the number of shanties, or *gecekondus,* has been increasing rapidly each year since the 1950s.

Throughout the 1970s the condition of the working class worsened. The decline in the rate of exploitation achieved as a result of the intense struggles in the late 1960s was sharply reversed after the 1971 coup: the rate increased from 331% in 1970 to 394% in 1972.[35] In 1973, it had reached 399%, and by the mid-1970s it was over 400%. The mass of surplus value increased from

12,118,705,000 T.L. in 1970 to 34,727,550,000 T.L. in 1973 – an increase of 187%.[36] The drive to squeeze out as much surplus value as possible from workers led to increased accidents at work. The number of work accidents rose from 144,731 in 1970 to 177,004 in 1973, to 201,000 in 1976. In addition, 4,129 workers were killed in work accidents between 1969 and 1974; and in the period 1974–79 this figure increased to 5,235.[37] However, the actual figures are much higher, as the data provided above include only insured workers, and therefore grossly underestimate the extent of accidents and deaths on the job.

Unemployment, too, reached disastrous levels during the 1970s, especially towards the end of the decade. There were 2 million unemployed in Turkey in 1971,[38] but by the end of 1978 this figure had reached 3.5 million or 20% of the labour force according to the OECD,[39] while official Turkish government sources estimate it to be close to 7 million![40] In addition, 400,000 persons are added to the work force every year, of which 165,000 are unable to find work and end up in the ranks of the unemployed.[41] The worsening economic situation in the latter half of the decade, which led to the industrial slump of the late 1970s, has driven many firms out of business and in the process left hundreds of thousands of workers jobless, thus compounding the unemployment problem:

> In Kayseri, the Chamber of Industry reported that 15 out of a total 30 workplaces, employing some 3,000 workers, had shut down. In Bursa, 117 firms shut down within the space of a year, leaving 10,000 jobless . . . [T]he famous state-owned Merinos Wool Mill employing over 3,000 workers is facing closure . . . Parallel to the closure of small and large firms, mass layoffs have become common practice. A survey by the Aegean Region Chamber of Industry reports that over 12,000 workers in the Izmir region lost their jobs in 11 months of 1978. The president of the Sosyal-Is trade union disclosed that 65,000 workers had been sacked in 1978. There are no signs that this trend will ease. MESS, the extremely reactionary employers' union in the metal industry, has warned that 350,000 workers could face the axe in the metal and automobile industries in the coming period [1979–80].[42]

It is within the context of this attack on the working class that the class struggle sharpened at the end of the 1970s.

The workers' response to the deteriorating economic situation has been the staging of mass strikes and demonstrations, factory occupations and open confrontation with the police and armed forces. Between 1970 and 1976 there occurred 658 industrial strikes, involving 101,815 workers.[43] By the mid-1970s, the size and strength of DISK and its associated unions had increased greatly and the workers' movement had become more militant and politicized. In September 1976, a general strike was called, demanding the elimination of the State Security Courts. In May 1977, 40,000 metal workers belonging to the Metal Workers Union (*Maden-Is*) began a historic strike against MESS, the reactionary employers' association, which lasted eight months and ended in victory for the metal workers.[44] Strikes and demonstrations intensified in 1978 with the March general strike against the fascist terror unleashed by the reactionary forces. On March 20, 1978, more than two million people took part in a two-hour general strike called by DISK, which quickly spread throughout the country, demonstrating the solidarity of huge numbers of workers, students, and progressives:

> At 8.00 a.m. on Monday morning [March 20] 650,000 DISK workers laid down their tools. Factories came to a halt, buses ceased running and teachers and students left their classrooms. Water and electricity were cut off in the capital city of Ankara. The strike and the 120,000-strong demonstration in Istanbul were supported not only by DISK, but also by some unions affiliated to *Turk-Is,* the Progressive Youth Organization (IGD), the Progressive Teachers' Association (TOB-DER) the Association of Progressive Lecturers (TUMOD), the Progressive Women's Association (IKD) and professional associations. Members of the Istanbul Bar held a protest demonstration in front of the Justice Building.
>
> The general strike and anti-fascist demonstrations spread beyond Ankara and Istanbul to Izmir, Bursa, Adana, Mersin, Hatay, and Gaziantep. More than 20,000 people took part in the Bursa demonstration.
>
> During the 2-hour general strike, workers hung great banners reading 'Fascism Shall Not Pass!' and 'Fascists Beware!' on the walls of their factories.[45]

On May Day 1977, and again in 1978, more than half a million workers, working people, progressives and revolutionaries marched to Istanbul's May Day Square for the largest May Day rally in the capitalist world. DISK, Maden Is, Tekstil, Bank-Sen, and TOB-DER were among the hundreds of trade unions and national and local organizations participating in these demonstrations.[46]

Such mass action, which demonstrated in concrete terms the unity, strength and militancy of the working class and its allies, opened a new chapter in the struggle of the Turkish working class, and other progressive forces against imperialism, the local collaborating bourgeoisie and their present-day fascist strike force, the NAP.

Class Struggle Intensifies – A Revolutionary Situation Develops

Workers' struggles, which began to intensify in the latter part of the 1970s, now reached a high level of political maturity. This was manifested in all the major rallies and demonstrations. The demands of the working class, under the leadership of its advanced, revolutionary contingents, were not restricted to narrow economic issues of the day, but were part and parcel of its long-term political interests that included the immediate struggle for the abolition of Articles 141 and 142, of the Constitution, withdrawal from NATO, and the legalization of the CPT.[47] Armed with organizational strength and a revolutionary outlook, the working class had thus become a major class force challenging the powers of the neo-colonial state. It is within this context that the fascist attacks began to intensify at the end of the 1970s.

The task of 'halting' the growing strength of the working class and its allies was given to Turkes and his fascist Nationalist Action Party (NAP) commandos.[48] The terror unleashed by the fascist forces claimed hundreds of lives during the latter part of the decade. From January to mid-December 1978, over 1,000 persons were killed by the fascist commandos. At the end of December 1978, escalation of fascist terror led to the bloodbath in Kahramanmaras where more than 100 persons were killed and over a thousand injured.[49] Following the massacre, martial law was declared in thirteen provinces, including Istanbul, Ankara, and eleven eastern provinces with a high proportion of Kurds.[50] In April 1979, another six eastern provinces, populated mainly by Kurds, were brought under martial law, bringing the number of provinces under Army control to nineteen. Martial law, imposed under the 'social democratic' Ecevit Government, greatly strengthened the hand of the reactionary forces, by putting tremendous power at the disposal of martial law commanders. As a result,

> In cities and villages all over the country, tens of progressive organizations and publications have been closed down . . . Soldiers and gendarmes *armed with machine-guns* are conducting daily searches at universities, schools, homes and factories. Students at Istanbul University are forced to pass through five check-points (manned by machine-gun toting soldiers) before entering classes. On 3 March 1979, *Milliyet* reported that all student dormitories in Istanbul were being searched.[51]

At the same time, attacks by the CIA-trained and equipped death squads of the fascist NAP intensified during 1979, bringing the death toll for 1978–79 to 2,500.[52] Bus, as Yurukoglu points out, 'Fascism in Turkey is not restricted to the NAP. Fascism is the choice of finance capital. The NAP is the present-day striking force of fascism.'[53] Through the use of the NAP storm-troopers and the imposition of martial law, the collaborating local bourgeoisie thus began laying the basis for an open fascist dictatorship.

In response to these attacks by the state and the fascist forces, the workers' struggle grew and intensified throughout this period. On December 30, 1978, nearly 30,000 people, from over 50 different organizations, marched against martial law and fascism in Izmir, demanding an end to martial law, the arrest of Turkes, and the closing down of the NAP. A week later, on January 5, 1979, all trade unions affiliated to DISK, the Confederation of Revolutionary Trade Unions, were joined by tens of thousands of teachers and working people in a five-minute stand in silence to protest against the fascist massacre in Kahramanmaras. Nearly one million working people stopped work throughout the country to take part in this successfully organized action. As May Day 1979 approached, the martial law commanders imposed a ban on all May Day meetings, demonstrations, and marches in the 19 provinces under martial law. On April 30, over 500 trade unionists and progressives, including the president of DISK and five members of its executive committee, were arrested. Following this, the Istanbul martial law authorities issued a statement announcing that a 29-hour curfew had been imposed, to take effect from midnight on Monday, April 30, to 5 a.m., Wednesday, May 2, 'warn[ing] the people of Istanbul . . . [that] all security forces under martial law command have the authority to shoot'.[54]

Despite the massive display of force by the police and armed forces, May Day meetings were held in all 19 provinces under martial law in a total of 43 cities and towns. In Istanbul 'at least 17 "pirate" May Day meetings were held in various parts of the city. Many of these at building sites, factories, and other work places were surrounded by troops and police armed with machine-guns. The defiant demonstrators were then taken to Inonu Stadium, which, after the style of the 1973 coup in Chile, had been turned into a concentration camp for the occasion. In all, at least 1,200 people were arrested . . . In Ankara, there were several clashes between security forces and demonstrators. Several people were wounded when police opened fire on one group. The arrests added up to 665. In Mersin, 198 people were arrested for carrying banners and shouting slogans in Kurdish.'[55] The most important of the 1979 May Day demonstrations, however, took place in Izmir:

> Due to the 29-hour curfew imposed on Istanbul, the traditional demonstration was held in Izmir. More than 100,000 people gathered in Konak Square, the heart of the city. Many thousands more were prevented from entering the city by roadblocks set up around the city by army and police. . .
>
> In addition to 10,000 police, also present [at the demonstration] were one gendarme commando unit and Aegean army command support units. 'Security' measures were even extended to the sea and the air as a number of gunboats stood ready in the harbour and helicopters circled overhead . . .
>
> Marchers began to gather in Konak Square as early as 5 a.m. The march was organized and led by *Maden-Is* (the Metal Workers Union)
>
> Alongside unions affiliated to the Confederation of Revolutionary Trade Unions (DISK) were several affiliated to the yellow *Turk-Is* Confederation . . .
>
> The participation in the march of hundreds of Kurdish democrats and progressives . . . was a rebuff to the stepped-up efforts to set Turk against Kurd . . .
>
> A Another important contingent of the march were the small peasants

> and rural workers represented by *Koy-Koop* (village co-operatives) and *Koy-Der* (the peasants association) . . .
>
> There was also massive and militant participation on the part of women organized in the Progressive Women's Organization . . .
>
> A high point of the demonstration occurred when thousands of IGD [Progressive Youth Organization] members from all over Turkey marched into Konak Square bearing red flags and shouting, 'Our road is the road of struggle of the working class!'[56]

Thus, despite martial law, May Day 1979, as in previous years, demonstrated once again the strength and unity of the workers' movement and showed the determination of the working class and its allies in the fight against the fascist and reactionary forces propped up by imperialism.

The struggle of the working class continued to intensify during the remainder of 1979 as thousands of workers at Maysan, Renault, and other nearby factories in Bursa clashed with military police.[57] In October, '400 workers occupied the Kula Textile Factory in Izmir . . . and 850 workers, 600 of them women, occupied the Ceyhan Textile Factory in Adana . . .'[58] At the end of December, strikes and demonstrations were held in more than 15 cities to protest military repression and in memory of the victims of the massacre in Kahramanmaras. The police opened fire on the demonstrators, killing a dozen students and teachers and wounding many more.[59] Over 4,000 people – workers, students, and teachers – were arrested and put into the country's stadiums; in Istanbul and Ankara alone, the number of arrested totalled 1,280 and 2,430 respectively.[60] Nearly 2,000 teachers were suspended because they boycotted classes on December 24 to take part in the demonstrations, and leaders of the Metal Workers Union (*Maden-Is*) and bank workers union (*Bank-Sen*) were arrested by the martial law authorities.[61] In Ankara, 'Martial law units were reinforced by special commando patrols, tanks, and armoured cars. In Istanbul, security forces set up roadblocks and the situation was explosive.'[62] In the capital, 'several hundred student demonstrators occupied the Yildirim Bayezit High School near Ankara University . . . Riot police moved in and firing [between students and police] continued for three hours . . . Another clash took place between students and security forces at the industrial vocational school opposite Ankara's central bank.'[63]

Strikes, factory occupations, student protests, and demonstrations continued in early 1980. In mid-January, workers in Izmir occupied the state-owned Taris thread factory, protesting the cancelling of their contracts by the Demirel Government and the dismissal of union leaders.[64] The occupation continued for a month. 'At one point in the Taris struggle, 35,000 workers from another union joined the action, which turned into a strong protest against the government's economic policy. Workers blocked the airport road, cut electricity, water, and transportation in some districts, and closed shops.'[65] In mid-February, thousands of troops stormed the plant and broke up the occupation. Some 1,500 workers were arrested after a six-hour seige.[66] A few days later, in Izmir, 'a march called by the left labour federation, DISK, to denounce the austerity measures developed into a two-day strike by 50,000 workers protesting the brutal action by thousands of troops, equipped with tanks and armoured cars, at the Taris thread factory.'[67] Also in February, 'in the capital city of Ankara . . . hundreds of students burned an effigy of Demirel and chanted, "No to the price rises!" Shops and offices in Istanbul were shut down for two days to protest the price hikes . . . In Izmir, three cops were killed and seven wounded in street battles with leftists as 2,500 police surrounded the Gultepe shantytown district and shelled it with tear gas bombs.'[68]

The economic and social crises of the late 1970s, and the acceleration of the working-class and people's struggle during the past year has led the ruling class to intensify repression and to look increasingly for an open fascist 'solution'. Alarmed by the growing workers' movement and the maturing revolutionary situation, the Turkish bourgeoisie is once again turning to the military for 'a way out' of the current crisis and the approaching civil war. Thus, in September 1980, a military coup led by the pro-NATO generals overthrew the right-wing civilian government of Suleyman Demirel and installed in its place an open fascist military dictatorship.

Turkey is in the midst of a major crisis that is driving the country toward civil war. The working class and its allies are strengthening their ranks and intensifying their struggle through armed confrontation with the state and the fascist forces in the factories, offices, schools, and streets. Frightened by the organized strength and high level of class consciousness of the working class and by the rapidly maturing revolutionary situation in Turkey, the collaborating bourgeoisie, becoming increasingly desperate, has installed an open fascist dictatorship. Well aware of the mounting fascist danger in Turkey, the working class, the revolutionary forces, progressives, and all other allies of the working class and people are waging a determined struggle to reverse this trend by smashing the forces of reaction acting on behalf of imperialism and the collaborating bourgeoisie. The following statement by *Maden-Is,* the Metal Workers Union, is clear evidence of the high level of consciousness and struggle of the working class of Turkey: 'This crisis', reads the statement, 'which arises from the capitalist system, from the ruling classes' policy of subservience to imperialism, is permanent and continuous . . . The way out of the crisis is through expelling imperialism and putting an end to the rule of the monopolies. We, the metal workers, are preparing for a great struggle against intense exploitation by the monopolies. This struggle is not separate from the struggle against imperialism and fascism.'[69]

Turkey is on the road to social revolution. But this will neither come easily nor of its own accord. Organization, party leadership and class alliances are crucial, and will, in the final analysis, determine whether the current historic confrontation between the bourgeoisie and the proletariat in Turkey will lead to socialism.

References

1. Martial Law Commander of Istanbul General Faik Turun's statement to the press is indicative of the military's conception of developments during 1970–71, when he said: 'We were on the verge of a civil war; this war had even begun. They called it "People's War" . . . Martial law was declared under these conditions.' Quoted in F. Ahmad, *The Turkish Experiment,* p. 321, f. 18.
2. The Turkish press reported 'rumours' of a meeting on March 11 between the commanders, Ambassador Handley, and Richard Helms, Director of the CIA, at the US Embassy in Ankara – thus implicating the CIA directly in the March 12 intervention. *Ibid.,* p. 265, f. 56.
3. These were: Ankara, Istanbul, Izmir, Zonguldak, Kocaeli, Sakarya, Eskisehir, Adana, Hatay, Diyarbakir, and Siirt.
4. J. Cousins, *Turkey: Torture and Political Persecution,* (London; Pluto Press, 1973), p. 6.
5. *Ibid.,* p. 7.
6. *Ibid.,* pp. 20–85.
7. The Republican People's Party (RPP) and the Justice Party (JP) are the two main bourgeois parties in Turkey. The former was originally organized by Ataturk in the early 1920s, and ruled Turkey throughout the period 1923–50. It advocated the development of a state capitalist economy based on state intervention in the economic sphere, while at the same time devising ways of improving the position of the weak Turkish national bourgeoisie. Its 'nationalistic' policies were intended to control and limit the power of foreign capital while simultaneously aiding the development of a 'self-centred' capitalism at home. Remaining within the capitalist world economy, however, it was only a matter of time as to when the party would be forced to develop policies that would return Turkey to the imperialist camp and allow its reintegration into the capitalist bloc. This came during and following World War II as Turkey succumbed to the growing power of the U.S. and to the NATO alliance. From the 1950s on, the position of the RPP and its leader Inonu has varied very little from the Democrat Party (DP) regime of Adnan Menderes. However, with the emergence of Bulent Ecevit as party leader and his 'left-of-centre' politics in the mid-1960s, the party began to give lip service to reforms and a return to the Kemalist policies of the 1930s, and was thus branded as 'social democratic'. The party has a broad 'nationalist', 'populist' and technocratic image and support base and is viewed by many Turks today as a party of bureaucratic 'reformers' interested in 'solving' Turkey's pressing economic problems 'in opposition to' the imperialist countries and within the framework of bourgeois democracy. Yet, during the course of its tenure in office in the late 1970s Ecevit and the RPP have *increased* Turkey's dependence on imperialism, enslaved the country to Western banks, and declared martial law in numerous provinces. Thus while Demirel and the right-wing Justice Party have always represented the reactionary aims of the Turkish comprador bourgeoisie, Ecevit and the RPP have taken up the role of a 'mediating force' in safeguarding the interests of that same class enemy.
8. C. Keyder, 'The Political Economy of Turkish Democracy' *New Left*

Review, No. 115 (May–June 1979), p. 40.
9. M. Howe, 'Ecevit Party Loses Majority in Turkey as Right Wing Gains', *The New York Times* (October 15, 1979), p.1.
10. Founded in 1961, OYAK became a large conglomerate in a short period of time, thanks to the requirement that regular officers in the armed forces must invest 10% of their salaries in the fund, to be reimbursed at a later date.
11. See 'The Army Conglomerate', *Time* (September 11, 1972), p. 73.
12. *Ibid.*
13. OYAK, *Onuncu Yil,* (Ankara, 1971); *Time* (September 11, 1972), p. 73.
14. Organisation for Economic Co-operation and Development (OECD), *Turkey,* p. 55.
15. *Ibid.,* and Turkiye Is Bankasi, *Review of Economic Conditions, 1979,* No. 4 (Ankara, 1979), p. 25.
16. OECD, *op. cit.,* p. 55.
17. *Ibid.*
18. *Euromoney* (June 1979), p. 45.
19. *Ibid.,* p. 49.
20. *Turkey Today,* No. 44 (March 1979), p. 7.
21. *Ibid.* According to *Euromoney* (June 1979), p. 42, after all the current rescheduling of the debt by the IMF and Western banks, Turkey would still have to pay between US$1.5 billion and US$2 billion in debt servicing alone each year until 1986.
22. The latest devaluation brings the value of the lira to US$1 = 70 T.L. as of January 1980. In 1975, it was US$1 = 15 T.L. The lira went through several devaluations in 1978 and 1979, and dropped in value to US$1 = 26 T.L. in March 1979 and US$1 = 47 T.L. in November 1979, until it fell to US$1 = 70 T.L. in January 1980. In the mid-1940s, however, the lira's value was nearly equal to that of the US $, when its rate was US$1 = 1.28 T.L. Even as late as in 1958, it was US$1 = 2.80 T.L., US$1 = 100 T.L. as of April 1981.
23. See *Guardian* (New York, (February 6, 1980), p. 12; and *Workers World* (January 4, 1980), p. 13.
24. Viewed from another vantage point, however, it could also be argued, as some left groups in Greece and Turkey have recently done, that, despite all the obvious advantages to the transnational monopolies and the devastating effects of this on the local economy and society, membership of the EEC by a country with a strong, organized, and class-conscious working class may well be the catalyst for the intensification of the class struggle within the Common Market, such that, in time, it would prepare the grounds for a *continent-wide* workers' movement that would raise the banner of the working class for a 'united socialist Europe'. This *unintended consequence* of European integration for monopoly profits is significant enough *in political terms* that its importance should not be underestimated.
25. State Institute of Statistics, *Statistical Pocket Book of Turkey, 1974,* (Ankara: S.I.S., 1975), pp. 68–9.
26. *Ibid.*
27. OECD, *op. cit.,* p. 31.
28. *Ibid.*

29. R. Yurukoglu, *Turkey – Weak Link of Imperialism*, p. 88. In the United States, 27% of workers were unionized in 1971, and in Italy 30%.
30. *Ibid.*
31. *Workers World* (January 4, 1980), p. 13.
32. With inflation running at 100% in 1979, the drop in real wages in 1979 is bound to be even bigger than that in 1978, for in following the IMF's 'recommendation' the government put a freeze on all wages and went on to propose in its 1979 budget a 40% cut in the real wages of workers employed in the public sector. See *Euromoney* (June 1979), p. 42.
33. R. Yurukoglu, *op. cit.*, p. 77.
34. However, the *official* minimum daily wage fixed for 1979–80 was 180 T.L.!
35. *Ibid.*, p. 59.
36. *Ibid.*, p. 154.
37. *Ibid.*, pp. 75–76; *Iscinin Sesi* (The Worker's Voice) (October 8, 1979), p. 15.
38. Commission on Employment and Manpower, *Report of the Special Commission on Employment and Manpower*, (Ankara, 1973), quoted in *Turkey Today*, No. 44 (March 1979), p. 17.
39. OECD data, quoted in *Ibid.*
40. Statement by the Minister of Social Security, quoted in *Ibid.*
41. *Report of the Special Commission*, quoted in *Ibid.*
42. 'Economy on the Brink,' *Turkey Today*, No. 44 (March 1979), p. 6.
43. International Labour Organization, *Yearbook of Labour Statistics, 1978*, (Geneva: ILO, 1978), p. 628.
44. *Turkey Today*, No. 35–36 (July–August 1978), p.11.
45. 'Two Million Take Part in General Strike Against Fascist Attacks', *Turkey Today*, No. 33–34 (May–June 1978), p. 12.
46. 'Half a Million Marched into May Day Square', *Ibid.*, pp. 4–6.
47. The Communist Party of Turkey, founded by Mustafa Suphi in 1920, was declared illegal in the early 1920s and has been forced to function clandestinely for all but the first two years of its existence. Despite the official ban, the Party has a substantial base and following throughout the country, especially among militant trade unions and progressive organizations.
48. The Nationalist Action Party (NAP), led by retired Colonel Alparslan Turkes, is one of the largest fascist organizations in Europe. A recent report on Turkes and his NAP characterizes him and his party as ultra-right, racist, and ruthless, adding that there was little difference between the power structure of the German Nazi Party and the Nationalist Action Party. Turkes established close ties with Nazi leaders in Germany in 1945 and has maintained his contacts to this day with the German Neo-Nazi underground. At the same time, he has expanded his network of contacts to include every important fascist, Nazi, and ultra-right leader and organization in the world. It is said that Turkes dreams of a vast empire of 'Greater Turkey' embracing all Turkic peoples, and stretching from Greece all the way to China. Recruiting its commando squads from Turkey's massive army of unemployed youth, the NAP has organized units of regimented, armed, terror gangs, called the 'Grey Wolves', that operate on a similar basis to Hitler's Brownshirts. In 1975, Turkes

became a vice-premier under Demirel and used his power to infiltrate the army, police, and social services with members of his party. As a result, members of the NAP are the only ones who can legally bear arms in Turkey. With the worsening of the economic crisis in Turkey in the latter half of the 1970s, the NAP has become the chief instrument of the Turkish ruling class 'to strike a blow' at the growing left and workers' movement aiming to 'reverse' the developing revolutionary situation in the country. Trained by the CIA and backed by Turkish military intelligence, the NAP commandos and their actions represent the last desperate efforts of the Turkish rulers to remain in power and safeguard their interests by attempting to preserve the crumbling neo-colonial system. It is in this context that the threat of fascism ought to be seen. It is also within this context that the recent military coup ought to be interpreted, and the objective role of the NAP fascists located in this latest crisis of dependent capitalism.

49. 'Massacre at Maras', *Turkey Today,* No. 42–43 (January–February 1979), p. 9.
50. The Kurds, one of several minority nationalities in Turkey, are the largest such group in the country. Concentrated mainly in the eastern provinces of Turkey, they now number nearly 9 million and make up 20 per cent of the population of Turkey.
51. 'Martial Law Heading for Open Fascist Dictatorship', *Turkey Today,* No. 44 (March 1979), p. 8.
52. J. Chediac, 'Turkey On the Road to Revolution', *Workers World* (February 22, 1980), p. 7. The 2,500 deaths in the past two years compares with 510 killed over the previous *decade.* In connection with the CIA's role in this context, S. Benhabib points out that: 'Former military prosecutor and Supreme Court Justice, Emin Deger, has detailed collaboration between the *Bozkurts* [the NAP commandos] and government counter-guerrilla units, and the close ties of the latter with the Central Intelligence Agency of the US. S. Benhabib, 'Right-wing Groups Behind Political Violence in Turkey', *MERIP Reports,* No. 77 (May 1979), p. 17.
53. R. Yurukoglu, *op. cit.,* p. 118.
54. 'Government Declares War on May Day', *Turkey Today,* No. 45–46 (April–May 1979), p. 7.
55. 'Istanbul Under Occupation', *Ibid,* p. 6.
56. 'May Day Triumphs Despite Martial Law', *Ibid.,* p. 4.
57. *Iscinin Sesi,* (The Workers' Voice), (December 17, 1979), p. 1.
58. 'Strikes, Occupations and Mass Arrests Characterize This Year's Collective Bargaining', *Turkey Today*, No. 48 (Fall 1979), p. 7.
59. J. Chediac, 'Turkish Government Brutally Suppresses Demonstrations', *Workers World,* (January 4, 1980), p. 13; *People's World* (January 5, 1980), p. 12, and (January 19, 1980), p. 12. Also, see *The New York Times* (December 25, 1979), p. A3.
60. *Ibid.*
61. *Ibid.* In retaliation against the teachers' boycott, on December 26 martial law authorities arrested 'an undisclosed number of teachers', closed down five schools, and banned the teachers' association (TOB-DER). See *The New York Times* (December 25, 1979), p. A3.

62. *Ibid.*
63. *Ibid.*
64. J. Chediac, 'Turkey on the Road to Revolution', *Workers World* (February 22, 1980), p. 7.
65. *Ibid.*
66. *Ibid.*
67. *Ibid.*
68. *Ibid.*
69. Quoted in *Turkey Today*, No. 48 (Fall 1979), p. 7.

8. Conclusion: The Approaching Civil War

Confronted with a highly class-conscious working class and a brewing revolutionary situation that threatened the very existence of the neo-colonial capitalist order, the Turkish bourgeoisie could no longer rule through the normal channels of political power. Direct control through military force remained the only option to 'halt' or 'dampen' the working class and people's movement mounting throughout the country. True to its neo-colonial nature, the military high command staged its coup and imposed matial law only after consultations with its foreign master in the headquarters of world imperialism. Thus, on September 3, 1980 – just nine days prior to the coup – General Tahsin Sahinkaya, head of Turkey's air force and now a junta member, arrived in Washington for high-level talks with U.S. officials. No doubt, of course, these talks centred around the deepening crisis in Turkey and the possible alternative moves by the Turkish state in response to the situation. It also comes as no surprise to see endorsements of the coup by NATO's overall commander, U.S. General Bernard Rogers, who visited Ankara four times in early October 1980, and General David Jones, Chairman of the U.S. Joint Chiefs of Staff, who visited Turkey in early November.[1]

These were followed by new loans extended to the government by a consortium of private multinational banks, totalling US$95 million, with an additional US$87 million from the World Bank.[2] Thus, a collapsing regime is being propped up by NATO, the U.S., and Western banks through a bloody 'military solution'.

The planned coup was carried out on September 12, 1980 by several top-ranking military commanders headed by General Kenan Evren. The leaders of the coup dissolved the National Assembly and dismissed Suleyman Demirel's government. The Prime Minister and his Cabinet were taken into custody, along with opposition leader Bulent Ecevit, more than one hundred parliamentary deputies and many trade union officials, students and intellectuals, including the head of the Istanbul Bar Association.[3] General Kenan Evren, Chief of Turkey's General Staff, was made Chairman of the new six-man ruling National Security Council (NSC), as the junta is formally called. On seizing power, one of the first actions of the generals was the extension of martial law to cover all 67 provinces to be in effect indefinitely. With the imposition of martial law throughout the country, the military commanders suspended the Constitution, dissolved Parliament, banned all political parties and outlawed political activity, banned all trade unions and strikes and held in custody over 500 of their leaders, ordered all striking workers (numbering 60,000) back to work, proposed to extend the working week to 56 hours, disbanded all professional and cultural organizations and other groups, closed down numerous newspapers and other publications, imposing strict censorship on the rest, took full control of Turkish Radio and Television (TRT), cancelled elections scheduled for the autumn of 1981, and amended the martial law code, granting unprecedented powers to the martial law commanders.[4]

The martial law regulations announced on September 21 included the following:

(1) Sentences handed down by Martial Law Courts will be double those previously handed down for the same offence; there will be no appeal against sentences involving less than three years' imprisonment; and fines will not be imposed as alternatives to prison sentences.

(2) Martial law commanders were authorized to place under surveillance all communications, including private letters; and to censor and/or ban any or all publications.

(3) They were authorized to control and/or ban all trade union and student activities, and to interrupt the course of education at any educational institution.

(4) Commanders may assume control over all public buildings, vehicles and management of personnel and strip any public servant of their duties when deemed necessary.

(5) Commanders may control the production, trade and distribution of all essential industrial and consumer goods.

(6) Security forces are authorized to shoot to kill persons not obeying their orders.

In addition to these powers accorded to the martial law commanders, the new legislation also stipulated that anyone failing to prove their identity upon request will face up to a year in goal and — even more extraordinary — cases being tried by martial law tribunals will continue to be heard by them even if martial law is lifted.[5]

The network of martial law control across the country was further extended and deepened by several other measures. On 26 September all elected mayors throughout the country were dismissed and municipal councils dissolved. The martial law commanders of each region began appointing new mayors and new councils. On 29 September, the National Security Council warned anyone in possession of bombs, dynamite, daggers, flick-knives, sword, scimitars, bayonets, throttling chain and cheese cutters to surrender them immediately. The penalty for possessing, carrying or selling any of these was stipulated as 30 years' imprisonment. At the end of October, it was announced that 160,000 weapons of the kind listed above had been handed in. On 12 October, the entire population of the country was confined indoors while a census was carried out. Census officers accompanied by two armed soldiers carried out house-to-house searches in every part of the country. The newspaper *Hurriyet* reported on October 14:

> Security forces carried out nationwide operations during the census, held in conditions of a curfew and many people wanted for various crimes were captured and detained. *People who refused to open their doors, although they were in, had their doors broken down.*[6]

In short, all democratic rights in Turkey have been abolished. People are searched at gunpoint in buses, at public gatherings, in the streets. Homes are entered without search warrants and family members taken away in army trucks. Those resisting arrest are taken to torture chambers and severely punished. The soldiers, the tanks and the police are everywhere. The people are ruled through terror. Fascism – the open military dictatorship of the moribund local and transnational bourgeoisie – reigns supreme. The workers and popular forces thus suffer a temporary setback.

The toll of this violence imposed on the Turkish workers and people has been and continues to be immense. Imprisonment, torture, and summary executions are the order of the day. Since the coup, more than 50,000 have been detained as of April 1981. They include workers, trade unionists, students, teachers, and other progressives. Thousands have been imprisoned and tortured, and dozens killed in torture chambers. Within just six days of the coup, it was reported in the Western press that some 10,000 persons had been detained since the generals had seized power.[7] This was in addition to the 46,000 detained during the six-month period October 1979 to May 1980.[8] According to the junta's own statements, the number of people detained since the coup runs into thousands: in a military communique on October 28, the junta announced that 11,500 persons had been detained since the coup.[9] And on December 25, the Martial Law Co-ordinating Committee announced in Ankara that, in the three-month period from September 10 to December 10, 29,995 people had been arrested, of whom 8,500 had already been indicted.[10] In the same period, 215 people were killed.[11] By early January 1981, over twenty people had been tortured to death. Moreover, courts-martial have condemned 108 people to be hanged, four of them have already been executed.[12] Among those who have been tortured and killed, while under detention since the coup, are: Ahmet Hilmi Feyzioglu, acting lawyer for the Bursa branch of the Metal Workers Union (Maden-Is), Rafet Demir, Zeynel Abidin Ceylan, Hasan Ozmen, Sadan Gazeteci, Ahmet Karlangac, Saadettin Guven, Zeki Yumurtaci, Mehmet Cizreli and Ilhan Erdost, whose bodies, according to reports received by Amnesty International, 'carried unmistakable signs of torture.'[13] The torture and murder of these activists is only one example of a whole series of brutalities carried out by the fascist regime in military prisons and police cells since the coup. Even before the coup, Amnesty reported that torture in Turkey is 'widespread and systematic'. Today the situation is even worse.

This terror, this violence imposed on the people through brute force, is, however, a sign of *weakness* – not strength – on the part of imperialism and its local collaborating agents. Under the leadership of the working class and its advanced, revolutionary contingents, the people's forces are gaining momentum. The struggle against the fascist dictatorship is intensifying. Everywhere people are voicing their opposition to military rule, and are seeking answers beyond bourgeois democracy, and toward socialism. A broad coalition of popular forces, under working-class leadership, is developing each passing day. While the working class and people's movement grows and expands under these difficult conditions, it is also clear that ruling circles are preparing to fight a long and bloody civil war – for the loss of Turkey to NATO and U.S. imperialism would be a heavy blow, unmatched since the Shah's overthrow in Iran. The situation in Turkey today points towards a massive confrontation between the forces of reaction and revolution. And it is becoming increasingly clear that the continuing revolutionary situation, which is unfolding under conditions of repressive military rule, will lead the country toward civil war and social revolution in the period immediately ahead.

References

1. Jim Paul, 'The Coup', *MERIP Reports*, No. 92 (January 1981), p. 4.
2. *Ibid*.
3. *Ibid*., p. 3.
4. See Kostic Kalioras, 'Turkey's Military Junta Wages War on Left', *Guardian* (New York), (February 11, 1981), p. 17 and *Turkey Today*, No. 53 (Autumn 1980).
5. 'Martial Law Rule is Arbitrary and Unrestricted', *Turkey Today*, No. 53 (Autumn 1980), p. 14. It should also be pointed out here that on September 21 the period for holding persons without charge was extended from 15 to 30 days and subsequently from 30 to 90 days.
6. *Ibid*.
7. *Financial Times*, (September 18, 1980).
8. Report released in Brussels in May 1980 by representatives of the World Federation of Trade Unions and the International Association of Democratic Lawyers, cited in *Turkey Today*, No. 53, p. 12.
9. The junta's official figures, however, are well below the actual numbers, as was admitted by *The New York Times*, mouthpiece of the U.S. bourgeoisie, when it reported that this figure had already reached 20,000 by early October! See *The New York Times*, (October 7, 1980), p. A2.
10. Kostic Kalioras, *op. cit*., p. 17.
11. *Ibid*.
12. *Ibid*.
13. According to the junta's official statements, some 'committed suicide while others 'jumped' from a fifth-floor window at Bursa police headquarters! Amnesty International, however, reports that they were

tortured continuously, many of them through the very last hours of their lives.

Bibliography

Ahmad, F. *The Young Turks: The Committee of Union and Progress in Turkish Politics, 1908-1914,* (London: Oxford University Press, 1969).

Ahmad, F. *The Turkish Experiment in Democracy, 1950-1975,* (Boulder: Westview Press, 1977).

Aksoy, A. (ed.) *Azgelismislik ve Emperyalizm,* (Underdevelopment and Imperialism), (Istanbul: Gozlem Yayinlari, 1975).

Alavi, H. 'The State in Post-Colonial Societies: Pakistan and Bangladesh', *New Left Review,* No. 74 (July 1972): 59-81.

Amin S. *Accumulation on a World Scale,* 2 Vols., (New York: Monthly Review Press, 1974).

Amin, S. *Unequal Development: An Essay on the Social Formations of Peripheral Capitalism,* (New York: Monthly Review Press, 1976).

Anderson, P. *Lineages of the Absolutist State,* (London: New Left Books, 1974).

Anderson, P. *Passages from Antiquity to Feudalism,* (London: New Left Books, 1974).

Andreyev, I. *The Noncapitalist Way,* (Moscow: Progress Publishers, 1977).

Ataov, T. *Amerika, NATO ve Turkiye,* (America, NATO and Turkey), (Ankara: Aydinlik, 1969).

Avcioglu, D. *Turkiye'nin Duzeni,* 2 Vols., (The Turkish Social Order), (Istanbul: Tekin Yayinevi, 1975).

Bairoch, P. *The Economic Development of the Third World Since 1900,* (Berkeley: University of California Press, 1975).

Baran, P. *The Political Economy of Growth,* (New York: Monthly Review Press, 1957).

Barbalet, J.M. 'Underdevelopment and the Colonial Economy', *Journal of Contemporary Asia,* Vol. 6, No. 2 (1976): 186-93.

Barkan, O. O. *Osmanli Imparatorlugunda Zirai Ekonominin Hukuki Esaslari,* (The Legal Bases of the Agrarian Economy in the Ottoman Empire), (Istanbul: Burhanettin Matbaasi, 1943).

Behramoglu, N. *Turkiye-Amerikan Iliskileri: Demokrat Parti Donemi,* (Turkish-American Relations: The Democratic Party Period), (Istanbul: Yar Yayinlari, 1973).

Berberoglu, B. 'Pre-Capitalist Modes of Production: Their Origin Contradictions, and Transformation', *Journal of Historical Research,* Vol. 21, No. 1 (1978): 62–80.

Berberoglu, B. and Landsberg, M. 'Transnational Production and the World-wide Contradictions of Advanced Capitalism', *Social Praxis,* Vol. 5,

Nos. 3-4 (1978): 181-205.
Berberoglu, B. 'Turkey: The Crisis of the Neo-colonial System', *Race & Class*, Vol. XXII, No. 3 (Winter 1981).
Berkes, N. *The Development of Secularism in Turkey*, (Montreal: McGill University Press, 1964).
Bettelheim, C. *Economic Calculation and Forms of Property*, (New York: Monthly Review Press, 1975).
Bhattacharya, D. 'Development and Technology in the Third World', *Journal of Contemporary Asia*, Vol. 6, No. 3 (1976): 314-22.
Bilen, I. 'Situation in Turkey', *World Marxist Review*, Vol. 22, No. 2 (February 1979); 35-47.
Blaisdell, D.C. *European Financial Control in the Ottoman Empire*, (New York, 1929).
Boratav, K. *Turkiye'de Devletcilik*, (Satism in Turkey), (Istanbul: Gercek Yayinevi, 1974).
Brown, M.B. *The Economics of Imperialism*, (Baltimore, MD: Penguine Books, 1974).
Cardoso, F.H. and Faletto, E. *Dependency and Development in Latin America*, (Berkeley: University of California Press, 1979).
Cavdar, T. (1970), *Osmanlilarin Yari-Somurge Olusu* (The Semi-Colonization of the Ottomans), (Istanbul: Ant Yayinlari, 1970).
Cavdar, T. (1973), 'Cumhuriyet Devri Baslarken Turkiye Ekonomisi', (The Turkish Economy at the Beginning of the Republican Era), in *Turkiye Ekonomisinin 50 Yili Semineri*, (Seminar on the 50 years of the Turkish Economy), (Bursa: I. ve T. I. Akademisi, 1973).
Cem, I. *Turkiye'de Geri Kalmisligin Tarihi*, (The History of Underdevelopment in Turkey), (Istanbul: Cem Yayinevi, 1970).
Demir, Y. 'Turkey in the Grip of Reaction', *World Marxist Review*, Vol. 6, No. 11 (November 1963): 20-27.
Derin, H. *Turkiye'de Devletcilik*, (Statism in Turkey), (Istanbul, 1940).
Divitcioglu, S. *Az Gelismis Ulkeler ve Asya Tipi Uretim Tarzi*, (Underdeveloped Countries and the Asiatic Mode of Production), (Istanbul: Elif Yayinlari, 1966).
Divitcioglu, S. *Asya Uretim Tarzi ve Osmanli Toplumu*, (The Asiatic Mode of Production and Ottoman Society), (Istanbul: Koz Yayinlari, 1971).
Divitcioglu, S. *Deger ve Bolusum*, (Value and Its Division), (Istanbul: I.U. Iktisat Fakultesi Yayini, 1976).
Dobb, M. *Studies in the Development of Capitalism*, (New York: International Publishers, 1963).
Dore, E., and Weeks, J. 'Class Alliances and Class Struggle in Peru', *Latin American Perspectives*, Vol. 4, No. 3 (Summer 1977): 4-17.
Earle, E.M. *Turkey, The Great Powers, and The Bagdad Railway: A Study in Imperialism*, (New York: Russell and Russell, 1966).
Emmanuel, A. *Unequal Exchange: A Study of the Imperialism of Trade*, (New York: Monthly Review Press, 1972).
Engels, F. *Anti-Duhring*, (New York: International Publishers, 1962).
Engels, F. *The Origin of the Family, Private Property and the State*, (New York: International Publishers, 1972).
Eren, N. *Turkey Today and Tomorrow*, (London: Pall Mall, 1961).
Ergil, D. (1974) 'Class Relations and the Turkish Transformation in Historical

Perspective', *Studia Islamica,* Fasicule XXXIX (1974).
Ergil, D. (1975), 'Class Conflict and Turkish Transformation', *Studia Islamica,* Fasicule XLI (1975).
Ergil, D. (1975) 'From Empire to Dependence; The Evolution of Turkish Underdevelopment', (Ph.D. dissertation, State University of New York at Binghamton, 1975).
Esping-Anderson, G., *et. al.* 'Modes of Class Struggle and the Capitalist State', *Kapitalistate,* Nos. 4-5 (Summer 1976): 186-220.
Farsoun, S., and Carroll, W.F. 'State Capitalism and Counterrevolution in the Middle East: A Thesis', in B. H. Kaplan (ed.), *Social Change in the Capitalist World Economy,* (Beverly Hills: Sage Publications, 1978).
Fernandez, R., and Ocampo, J. 'The Andean Pact and State Capitalism in Colombia', *Latin American Perspectives,* Vol. II, No. 3 (Fall 1975): 19-35.
Fisek, K. 'Osmanli Dis Borclari Ustune, (On Ottoman External Debts)„ *Siyasal Bilgiler Fakultesi Dergisi,* XXII, 3 (1968).
Fisek, K. *Turkiye'de Kapitalizmin Gelismesi ve Isci Sinifi,* (The Development of Capitalism and the Working Class in Turkey), (Ankara: Dogan Yayinevi, 1969).
Frank, A.G. *Capitalism and Underdevelopment in Latin America,* (New York: Monthly Review Press, 1969).
Frank, A.G. *Lumpenbourgeoisie: Lumpendevelopment,* (New York: Monthly Review Press, 1972).
Frey, F.W. *The Turkish Political Elite,* (Cambridge, MA: The M.I.T. Press, 1965).
Gandy, D.R. *Marx and History,* (Austin: University of Texas Press, 1979).
Gerstein, I. 'Theories of the World Economy and Imperialism', *Insurgent Sociologist,* Vol. 7, No. 2 (Spring 1977): 9-22
Goldfrank, W. (ed). *The World System of Capitalism: Past and Present,* (Beverly Hills: Sage Publications, 1979).
Halliday, F. 'The Arc of Revolutions: Iran, Afghanistan, South Yemen, Ethiopia', *Race & Class,* Vol. XX, No. 4 (Spring 1979): 373-90.
Harding, T.F. 'Dependency, Nationalism and the State in Latin America', *Latin American Perspectives,* Vol, III, No. 4 (Fall 1976): 3-11.
Harris, G.S. 'The Role of the Military in Turkish Politics', *Middle East Journal,* Vol. 19, Nos. 1-2 (Winter-Spring 1965): 54-66 and 169-76.
Hayter, T. *Aid as Imperialism,* (Baltimore, MD: Penguin Books, 1971).
Hershlag, Z. Y. *Turkey: The Challenge of Growth,* (Leiden: E.J. Brill, 1968).
Hindess, B., and Hirst, P.Q. *Pre-Capitalist Modes of Production,* (London: Routledge and Kegan Paul, 1975).
Hindess, B., and Hirst, P.Q. *Mode of Production and Social Formation,* (London: The Macmillan Press, 1977).
Hilton, R. (ed.) *The Transition from Feudalism to Capitalism,* (London: New Left Books, 1976).
Hussein, M. *Class Conflict in Egypt: 1945-1970,* (New York: Monthly Review Press, 1973).
Inalcik, (1964), 'The Nature of Traditional Society: Turkey', in R.E. Ward and D.A. Rustow (eds.), *Political Modernization in Japan and Turkey,* (Princeton: Princeton University Press, 1964).
Inalcik, H. 'Capital Formation in the Ottoman Empire', *Journal of Economic*

History, Vol. 29, No. 1 (March 1969): 97-140.
Inalcik, H. *The Ottoman Empire*, (New York: Praeger Publishers, 1973).
International Bank for Reconstruction and Development, (1951), *The Economy of Turkey: An Analysis and Recommendations for a Development Program*, (Baltimore: The Johns Hopkins Press, 1951).
IBRD, (1973), *Turkey: Prospects and Problems of an Expanding Economy*, (Washington, DC: World Bank, 1973).
International Labour Organization, *Labour Problems in Turkey*, (Geneva: International Labour Office, 1950).
ILO, *Yearbook of Labour Statistics*, annual (Geneva: International Labour Office, 1943-1978).
Islamoglu, H., and Faroqhi, S. 'Crop Patterns and Agricultural Production Trends in Sixteenth-Century Anatolia', *Review*, Vol. II, No. 3 (Winter 1979): 401-36.
Issawi, C. (ed.) *The Economic History of the Middle East*, (Chicago: University of Chicago Press, 1966).
Kalioras, K. 'Turkey's Military Junta Wages War On Left', *Guardian* (New York), (11 February 1981).
Kaplan, B.D. (ed.) *Social Change in the Capitalist World Economy*, (Beverly Hills: Sage Publications, 1978).
Karadeniz, H. *Kapitalsiz Kapitalistler*, (Capitalists Without Capital), (Istanbul: Vardiya Yayinlari, 1977).
Karpat, K.H. *Turkey's Politics: The Transition to a Multi-party System*, (Princeton: Princeton University Press, 1959).
Karpat, K.H., 'Social Effects of Farm Machinization in Turkish Villages', *Social Research*, Vol. 27, No. 1 (Spring 1960): 83-103.
Karpat, K.H. 'The Military and Politics in Turkey, 1960-64', *American Historical Review*, Vol. 75, No. 6 (October 1970): 1954-83.
Kay, G. *Development and Underdevelopment: A Marxist Analysis*, (New York; St. Martin's Press, 1975).
Keyder, C. 'The Dissolution of the Asiatic Mode of Production', *Economy and Society*, Vol. 5, No. 2 (May 1976): 178-96.
Keyder, C. *Emperyalizm, Azgelismislik ve Turkiye*, (Imperialism, Underdevelopment and Turkey), (Istanbul: Birikim Yayinlari, 1976).
Keyder, C. 'The Political Economy of Turkish Democracy', *New Left Review*, No. 115 (May-June 1979): 3-44.
Kivilcimli, H. *Turkiye'de Isci Sinifinin Sosyal Varligi*, (The Social Condition of the Working Class in Turkey), (Istanbul, 1935).
Kivilcimli, H. *Turkiye'de Kapitalizm*, (Capitalism in Turkey), (Istanbul, 1965)
Kivilcimli, H. *27 Mayis ve Yon Hareketinin Sinifsal Elestirisi*, (Class Analysis of the 27 May and Yon Movements), (Istanbul, 1970).
Kongar, E. *Turkiye'nin Toplumsal Yapisi*, (The Social Structure of Turkey), Istanbul: Cem Yayinevi, 1976).
Koymen, A. *Ortak Pazar Gercegi ve Turkiye'nin Sanayilesme Sorunu*, (The Common Market and the Question of Turkey's Industrialization), (Istanbul: Yar Yayinlari, 1974).
Krader, L. *The Asiatic Mode of Production: Sources, Development and Critique in the Writings of Karl Marx*, (Assem: Van Gorcum, 1975).
Krueger, A.O., *Turkey*, (New York: National Bureau of Economic Research, 1974).

Kurmus, O. *Emperyalizmin Turkiye'ye Girisi,* (The Penetration of Imperialism into Turkey), (Istanbul: Bilim Yayinlari, 1974).

Land, J.W. 'The Role of the Government in the Economic Development of Turkey, 1923 to 1963', *Rice University Program of Development Studies,* Paper No. 8 (Fall 1970).

Lenin, V.I. *Imperialism, The Highest Stage of Capitalism,* (New York: International Publishers, 1970).

Lenin, V.I. *State and Revolution,* (New York: International Publishers, 1971)

Lenin, V.I. *Collected Works,* 45 Vols, (Moscow: Foreign Languages Publishing House, 1960-70).

Lewis, B. *The Emergence of Modern Turkey,* 2nd edition (New York: Oxford University Press, 1968).

Longuenesse, E. 'The Class Nature of the State in Syria', *MERIP Reports,* No. 77 (May 1979): 3-11.

Magdoff, H. *Imperialism: From the Colonial Age to the Present,* (New York: Monthly Review Press, 1978).

Malik, A. 'Inflation and Monetary Policy in Turkey: 1950-1961' (Ph.D. dissertation, The American University, 1964).

Mandel, E. *Marxist Economic Theory,* (London: Merlin Press, 1968).

Mandel, E. *Late Capitalism,* (London: New Left Books, 1975).

Mardin, S. 'Historical Determinants of Stratification: Social Class and Class Consciousness in Turkey', *Siyasal Bilgiler Fakultesi Dergisi,* Vol. XXII, No. 4 (December 1967): 110-142.

Marx, Karl. *The Eighteenth Brumaire of Louis Bonaparte,* (New York: International Publishers, 1963).

Marx, Karl, *Pre-Capitalist Economic Formations,* (New York: International Publishers, 1964).

Marx, Karl. *Capital,* 3 Vols. (New York: International Publishers, 1967).

Marx, Karl. *Grundrisse: Foundations of the Critique of Political Economy,* (London: New Left Books and Penguin, 1973).

Marx, K. and Engels, F. *On Colonialism*, (New York: International Publishers, 1972).

Marx, K. and Engels, F. *Collected Works*, 12 Vols. (New York: International Publishers, 1975).

McFarlane, B. 'Imperialism in the 1980s', *Journal of Contemporary Asia,* Vol. 7, No. 4 (1977): 453-61.

McMichael, P. 'The Concept of Primitive Accumulation: Lenin's Contribution', *Journal of Contemporary Asia,* Vol. 7, No. 4 (1977): 497-512.

McMichael, P., *et. al.* 'Imperialism and the Contradictions of Development', *New Left Review,* No. 85 (May-June 1974): 83-104.

Middle East Research and Information Project, 'Turkey: The Generals Take Over', *MERIP Reports,* No. 93 (January 1981).

Ministry of Economy, Industrial Research Commission, *2 inci 5 Yillik Sanayi Plani,* (Second Five Year Industrial Plan), (Ankara: Basvekalet Matbaasi, 1936).

Ministry of Foreign Affairs, *Quarterly Report on the Marshall Plan in Turkey,* (Ankara: Basvekalet Matbaasi, 1951).

Ministry of Interior, *Turkey on the Way of Industrialization,* (Ankara: Basvekalet Matbaasi, 1937).

MI. *The Development of National Banking in Turkey,* (Ankara: Basvekalet

Matbaasi, 1938).
Ministry of Reconstruction and Resettlement (MRR), General Directorate of Housing, *Urbanization, Squatter Houses and Housing Policy,* (Ankara: Dogus Ltd. Sti. Matbaasi, 1966).
MRR, General Directorate of Housing, *Gecekondus in Ankara,* (Ankara: Dogus Ltd. Sti Matbaasi, 1966).
MRR. *Gecekondus in Ankara-Gulveren,* (Ankara: Dogus Ltd. Sti Matbaasi, 1966).
MRR. *Izmir Gecekondulari,* (Ankara: Dogus Ltd. Sti Matbaasi, 1966).
MRR. *Les Bidonvilles d'Istanbul,* (Ankara: Dogus, Ltd. Sti Matbaasi, 1966).
Moore, B. *The Social Origins of Dictatorship and Democracy,* (Boston: Beacon Press, 1966).
Morgil, O. 'The Social Structure and Economic Development of Turkey, 1950-1960', (Ph. D. dissertation, University of California at Riverside, 1972).
Nabudere, D. *The Political Economy of Imperialism,* (London: Zed Press, 1978).
Nalbandoglu, R. 'Turkiye'de Ziraat Iscilerinin Durumu', (The Condition of Agricultural Workers in Turkey), *Ictimai Siyaset Konferanslari,* I. Kitap (Istanbul: Iktisat Fakultesi Yayinlari, 1948).
Neyzi, N. 'The Middle Classes in Turkey', in K.H. Karpat (ed.), *Social Change and Politics in Turkey,* (Leiden: E.J. Brill, 1973).
Novichev, A.D. 'The Development of Agriculture in Anatolia', in C. Issawi (ed.), *The Economic History of the Middle East,* (Chicago: University of Chicago Press, 1966).
Orta Dogu Teknik Universitesi (ODTU), Idari Ilimler Fakultesi Orgenciler Dernegi, *Cok Uluslu Sirketler ve Turkiye,* (Multinational Corporations and Turkey), (Ankara: Asimlar Matbaasi, 1976).
Okan, H., and Y. Demir 'Turkey: Ways of Development', *World Marxist Review,* Vol. 8, No. 5 (May 1965): 62-68
Okcun, A.G. *Turkiye Iktisat Kongresi, 1923-Izmir,* (Economic Congress of Turkey, 1923 Izmir), (Ankara: Siyasal Bilgiler Fakultesi Yayinlari, 1968).
Okyar, O. 'Industrialization in Turkey', *Middle Eastern Affairs,* Vol. IV, No. 6-7 (June-July 1953): 209-17.
Okyar, O. 'The Concept of Etatism', *Economic Journal,* No. 297 (March 1965).
Organization for Economic Co-operation and Development (OECD), Economic Surveys, *Turkey,* (Paris: OECD, 1978).
Organization for European Economic Co-operation (OEEC), *1955 Economic Conditions in Turkey,* (Paris: OEEC, 1956).
OEEC, *1951-58 Bulletins statistiques de l'OECE. Commerce exterieur, Serie 4: Turquie,* (Paris: OEEC, 1951 to 1958).
OEEC, *The Work of the Conference on Financial Asssitance to Turkey and on Turkish Debts,* (Paris: OEEC, 1959).
Orhan, B. *Dix Annees de Regime Republicain,* (Istanbul, 1933).
Oz, D. 'Fascist Escalation Continues', *Turkey Today,* Nos. 33-34 (May-June 1978).
Ozbudun, E. *The Role of the Military in Recent Turkish Politics,* (Cambridge, MA: Harvard University, Center for International Affairs, 1966).

Ozeken, A.A. 'Turkiye'de Sanayi Iscileri', (Industrial Workers in Turkey), *Ictimai Siyaset Konferanslari,* 1. Kitap (Istanbul: Iktisat Fakultesi Yayinlari, 1948).

Ozgur, O. (1972), *Turkiye'de Kapitalizmin Gelismesi,* (The Development of Capitalism in Turkey), (Istanbul: Gercek Yayinevi, 1972).

Ozgur, O. (1976) *Sanayilesme ve Turkiye,* (Industrialization and Turkey), (Istanbul: Gercek Yayinevi, 1976).

Payer, C. *The Debt Trap: The International Monetary Fund and the Third World,* (New York: Monthly Review Press, 1974).

Petras, J. 'State Capitalism and the Third World', *Journal of Contemporary Asia,* Vol. 6, No. 4 (1976): 432-43.

Petras, J. *Critical Perspectives on Imperialism and Social Class in the Third World,* (New York: Monthly Review Press, 1978).

Pfeifer, K. 'State Capitalism and Development', *MERIP Reports,* No. 78 (June 1979): 3-11.

Popov, Y. *The Developing Countries from the Standpoint of Marxist Political Economy,* (Moscow: Progress Publishers, 1977).

Poulantzas, N. *Political Power and Social Classes,* (London: New Left Books, 1973).

Poutantzas, N. *Fascism and Dictatorship,* (London: New Left Books, 1974).

Poulantzas, N. *State, Power, Socialism,* (London: New Left Books, 1978).

Roberts, B. *Cities of Peasants: The Political Economy of Urbanization in the Third World* (Beverley Hills: Sage Publications, 1979).

Rodney, W. *How Europe Underdeveloped Africa,* (Dar es Salaam: Tanzania Publishing House, 1972).

Rosen, S.M. 'Labor in Turkey's Economic Development', (Ph.D. dissertation, Massachusetts Institute of Technology, 1960).

Rozaliev, Y.N. *Turkiye Sanayi Proletaryasi* (The Turkish Industrial Proletariat), (Istanbul: YarYayinlari, 1974).

Sayan, K. 'Turkish Etatism with Special Reference to the Textile Industry in Turkey,' (Ph. D. dissertation, University of Pennsylvania, 1968).

Selik, M. *Turkiye'de Yabanci Ozel Sermaye, 1923-1960,* (Foreign Private Capital in Turkey, 1923-1960), (Ankara: Siyasal Bilgiler Fakultesi, 1961).

Sencer, O. *Turkiye'de Isci Sinifi,* (The Working Class in Turkey), (Istanbul: Habora Yayinevi, 1969).

Serin, N. '1923' ten Bu Yana Turkiye'nin Sanayilesme Siyaseti' (Turkey's Politics of Industrialization Since 1923), *Siyasal Bilgiler Fakultesi Dergisi*, (June 1965).

Sertel, Y. *Turkiye'de Ilerici Akimlar,* (Progressive Movements in Turkey), (Istanbul: Ant Yayinlari, 1969).

Sertel, Y. 'The Problem of Development in the Third World and the Kemalist Experience', *Development and Socio-Economic Progesss,* Vol. I, No. 1 (November 1977): 57-68.

Shivji, I. *Class Struggles in Tanzania,* (New York: Monthly Review Press, 1976).

Solodovnikov, V., and Bogoslovsky, V. *Non-Capitalist Development*, (Moscow: Progress Publishers, 1975).

Sonmez, N. *Existing Land Ownership and Land Use Conditions in Turkey,* (Ankara: Ankara University Press, 1964).

Stalin, J.V. *Marxism and the National Question,* (New York: International Publishers, 1942).
Stalin, J.V. *Works,* 13 Vols., (Moscow: Foreign Languages Publishing House, 1953).
Stallings, B. *Economic Dependency in Africa and Latin America,* (Beverly Hills: Sage Publications, 1972).
State Institute of Statistics, *1950 Census of Agriculture,* (Ankara: SIS, 1953).
SIS. *1960 Housing Conditions – Survey in 20 Cities*, (Ankara: SIS, 1962).
SIS. *Summary of Agricultural Statistics, 1936-1956,* (Ankara: Devlet Istatistik Enstitusu Matbaasi, 1967).
SIS. *National Income and Expenditure of Turkey, 1948-1972*, (Ankara: Devlet Istatistik Entitusu Matbaasi, 1973).
SIS. *Turkiye'de Toplumsal ve Ekonomik Gelismenin 50 Yili,* (50 Years of Social and Economic Development in Turkey), (Ankara: Devlet Istatistik Enstitusu Matbaasi, 1973).
SIS. *Tarim Istatistikleri Ozeti,* (Summary of Agricultural Statistics), (Ankara: Devlet Istatistik Enstitusu Matbaasi, 1973).
SIS. *Census of Industry and Business Establishments, 1970*, (Ankara: Devlet Istatistik Enstitusu Matbaasi, 1973).
SIS. *Annual Survey of the Manufacturing Industry, 1973,* (Ankara: Devlet Istatistik Enstitusu Matbaasi, 1974).
SIS. *Agricultural Structure and Production,* (Ankara: Devlet Istatistik Enstitusu Matbaasi, 1975).
SIS. *Annual Foreign Trade Statistics,* (Ankara: Devlet Istatistik Enstitusu Matbaasi, 1975).
SIS. *Statistical Yearbook of Turkey* (Ankara: Devlet Istatistik Enstitusu Matbaasi, annual).
State Planning Organization, *Development Plan, First Five Years (1963-1967), 1964 Annual Programme,* (Ankara: Devlet Planlama Teskilati, 1963).
SPO. *Development Plan, First Five Years (1963-1967), 1965 Annual Programme,* (Ankara: Devlet Planlama Teskilati, 1964).
SPO. *Introducing Turkey's State Planning Organization,* (Ankara: Devlet Planlama Teskilati, 1963).
SPO. *A Survey on Foreign Capital Investment in Turkey,* (Ankara: Devlet Planlama Teskilati, 1964).
Sutcliffe, R.B. *Industry and Underdevelopment,* (London: Addison-Wesley Publishing Co., 1971).
Sutcliffe, R.B. 'Imperialism and Industrialization in the Third World', in B. Sutcliffe and R. Owen (eds.), *Studies in the Theory of Imperialism,* (London: Longman, 1972).
Szentes, T. *The Political Economy of Underdevelopment,* (Budapest: Akademiai Kiado, 1971).
Szymanski, A. 'Capital Accumulation on a World Scale and the Necessity of Imperialism', *Insurgent Sociologist,* Vol. 7, No. 2 (Spring 1977): 35-53.
Szymanski, A. *The Capitalist State and the Politics of Class,* (Cambridge, MA: Winthrop, 1978).
Sweezy, P. *The Theory of Capitalist Development,* (New York: Monthly Review Press, 1942).

Tekeli, I. and Ilkin, S. *1929 Dunya Buhraninda Turkiye'nin Iktisadi Politika Arayislari,* (Turkey's Search for Political Economic Solutions During the 1929 World Crisis), (Ankara: Orta Dogu Teknik Universitesi, 1977).

Therborn, G. *What Does the Ruling Class Do When It Rules?,* (London: New Left Books, 1978).

Trimberger, E.K. 'State Power and Modes of Production', *Insurgent Sociologist,* Vol. 7, No. 2 (Spring 1977): 85-98.

Trimberger, E.K. *Revolution from Above: Military Bureaucrats and Development in Japan, Turkey, Egypt, and Peru,* (New Brunswick, NJ: Transaction Books, 1978).

Tuna, O. 'Trade Unions in Turkey', *International Labor Review,* (November 1964): 413-31.

Tuncer, B. *Turkiye'de Yabanci Sermaye Sorunu,* (The Question of Foreign Capital in Turkey), (Ankara: Siyasal Bilgiler Fakultesi Yayinlari, 1968).

Tunckanat, H. *Ikili Anlasmalarin Icyuzu,* (The Essence of Bilateral Agreements), (Istanbul: Tekin Yayinevi, 1975).

Turk, I. *Turk Toplumunda Sosyal Siniflar,* (Social Classes in Turkish Society), (Istanbul: Oncu Kitabevi, 1970).

Ulyanovsky, R. *On Some Questions of the Non-Capitalist Development of the Countries of Asia and Africa,* (Moscow: Progress Publishers, 1969).

United Nations, *Yearbook of National Accounts Statistics,* (New York: United Nations, annual).

U.N. *Yearbook of International Trade Statistics,* (New York: United Nations, annual).

U.N. *Demographic Yearbook,* (New York: United Nations, annual).

U.N. Industrial Development Organization, *World Industry Since 1960: Progress and Prospects,* (New York: United Nations, 1979).

Union of Turkish Progressives in Britain, 'Junta Tries to Veil Fascism', *Turkey Today,* No. 53 (Autumn 1980).

United States, Agency for International Development, *Economic and Social Indicators-Turkey,* (Ankara: A.I.D., 1965).

U.S. *A.I.D. Economic Data Book: Near East and South Asia,* (Washington: A.I.D., 1968).

U.S. Department of Commerce, *Investment in Turkey,* (Washington: Government Printing Office, 1956).

U.S. Department of Commerce, *Basic Data on the Economy of Turkey,* (Washington: Government Printing Office, 1966).

U.S. Department of Labor, Bureau of Labor Statistics, *Labor Law and Practice in Turkey,* (Washington: Government Printing Office, 1963).

U.S. Department of State, *Turkey: Handbook of Economic Statistics,* (Washington: Government Printing Office, 1948).

Varlik, B. *Turkiye'de Sermaye'nin Tesviki,* (The Encouragement of Industry in Turkey), (Ankara: O.D.T.U. Idari Ilimler Fakultesi Ogrenci Dernegi Yayinlari, 1976).

Wallerstein, I. *The Modern World System,* (New York: Academic Press, 1974)

Wallerstein, I. *The Capitalist World Economy,* (Cambridge: Cambridge University Press, 1979).

Wallerstein, I. 'The Ottoman Empire and the Capitalist World Economy', *Review,* Vol. II, No. 3 (Winter 1979): 389-98.

Ward, R.E. and D.A. Rustow (eds.) *Political Modernization in Japan and Turkey*, (Princeton: Princeton University Press, 1964).

Warren, B. 'Imperialism and Capitalist Industrialization', *New Left Review*, No. 81 (September-October 1973): 3-44.

Warren, B. *Inflation and Wages in Underdeveloped Countries: India, Peru and Turkey, 1939-1960*, (London: Frank Cass, 1977).

Weiker, W. *The Turkish Revolution 1960-1961*, (Washington, DC: The Brookings Institution, 1963).

Wittfogel, K.A. *Oriental Despotism: A Comparative Study of Total Power*, (New Haven: Yale University Press, 1957).

Yurukoglu, R. *Turkey – Weak Link of Imperialism*, (London: Iscinin Sesi Publications, 1979).

Index